HANDWRITING 2

Second Edition

Charlene Killian

Karen L. Wolff

Joyce Garland

Teacher's Edition

bju press®

Greenville, South Carolina

NOTE:

The fact that materials produced by other publishers may be referred to in this volume does not constitute an endorsement of the content or theological position of materials produced by such publishers. Any references and ancillary materials are listed as an aid to the student or the teacher and in an attempt to maintain the accepted academic standards of the publishing industry.

HANDWRITING 2 Teacher's Edition
Second Edition

Developed by
Charlene Killian
Karen L. Wolff

Revision Coordinator
Joyce Garland

Editor
Martin Grove

Revision Graphics Coordinator
Dick Mitchell

Illustrators
Johanna Berg
J. Drew Conley
Timothy Davis
Barbara Gladin
Robert Martin
Mark Mulfinger
Lynda Slattery
Del Thompson
Stephanie True

Graphics
Holly Gilbert
Chris Hartzler
Brian Johnson
Duane Nichols

Computer Formatting
Peggy Hargis

© 1998 BJU Press
Greenville, South Carolina 29609
First Edition © 1982 BJU Press

ISBN 978-1-57924-105-6

15 14 13 12 11 10

Contents

Introduction v

Historical background v

Rationale for development of BJU Press PreCursive and cursive handwriting v

    The PreCursive alphabet v

    The cursive alphabet vi

    Stroke formations vii

Teaching handwriting xiv

    Teacher attitudes xiv

    Seating arrangements xiv

    Desk position and posture xiv

    Paper position xiv

    Pencil hold xiv

    Handwriting paper xiv

    Writing at the chalkboard xiv

    Special handwriting problems xv

Letter formation xv

    Letter alignment xv

    Slant of letters xv

    Spacing xv

    Neatness xvi

    Rhythm xvi

Evaluation of handwriting xvi

    Student evaluation xvi

    Teacher evaluation xvi

Developing handwriting consciousness xvii

    Displaying students' handwriting xvii

    Other classroom activities using handwriting xvii

Objectives xviii

Lessons 1

Appendix A1

Glossary A23

Introduction

Good handwriting is an essential skill—a form of expression and communication. Because handwriting is a complex process that requires a coordinated effort of nearly five hundred muscles, instruction should begin in kindergarten and continue through the elementary grades. Accordingly, *HANDWRITING 2 for Christian Schools* seeks to lay a foundation of writing skills on which early learnings are broadened and reinforced, not replaced, and to provide proper motivation throughout the elementary grades.

Historical background

Handwriting instruction reflects the vacillating pendulum of educational philosophy. Teachers in the past spent much time instructing their students in the "whole-arm" technique, popular in the latter part of the nineteenth century. Using this technique, the writer's whole arm moved from the shoulder as he wrote. This movement proved extremely difficult for beginning elementary children whose coordination was not sufficiently developed for this technique. Thus when teachers began lessons in cursive ("running" or "connected" writing), they also began endless handwriting drills.

And since this technique assumed teaching cursive in the first grade, children had to learn two alphabets—a cursive alphabet for writing and a typeface alphabet for reading.

The twentieth-century response to this technique was twofold. Some teachers eagerly embraced a partial solution—the manuscript alphabet, introduced in 1921. This alphabet, because it looked more like the typeface the students were expected to read, eliminated the necessity of having the students learn two alphabets in first grade. Moreover, since this alphabet took less time to teach and required fewer drills, it rapidly became accepted as the best method for teaching children to write. Other teachers, weary of handwriting drills, stopped teaching handwriting altogether. They argued that students could learn handwriting skills through observation.

Although the manuscript alphabet is popularly accepted today by many educators, it is becoming increasingly apparent throughout the educational system that the manuscript style has several fundamental problems. First, because the letters consist of sticks and circles, children have difficulty forming the letters properly. Making straight stick shapes and making round circle shapes are unnatural movements for the writing hand. Forming these shapes properly demands careful drawing motions. Second, children have difficulty remembering where to put the stick in relation to the circle. Many manuscript *b*s become *d*s and many *p*s become *q*s when a child cannot remember on which side of the circle the stick belongs. In addition, connecting the circle and the stick properly requires well-developed motor skills and careful drawing motions.

Third, since most of the letters bear little resemblance to the cursive letters taught later, students must learn a completely different system of movements to form cursive letters. In no other subject is such a drastic change common practice. On the contrary, early skills usually provide the foundation for further and more advanced skill development.

Rationale for development of BJU Press PreCursive and cursive handwriting

In developing *HANDWRITING for Christian Schools*, Bob Jones University Press followed the guidelines of research to bring the instructional philosophy into balance.

The PreCursive alphabet

This alphabet corrects the problems inherent in the traditional manuscript and cursive alphabets while retaining the advantages.

1. The PreCursive letters look very much like the letters children see in their reading materials.
2. The PreCursive alphabet capitalizes on the natural movements of a young child's writing hand. Oval shapes replace circles and slanted lines replace the vertical lines. Rather than drawing, a child begins early to develop a

rhythm and a flow that will minimize the transition to cursive writing.

3. Twenty-two of the PreCursive lowercase letters and seventeen of the PreCursive uppercase letters require only one stroke. Fewer stops and starts and decisions aid the child in remembering how to write the letters; a byproduct of this is fewer reversals. Again the transition to cursive writing is aided.

The cursive alphabet

The specific letter styles adapted for the cursive letters in the Handwriting program were chosen according to the following criteria:

    1. Legibility was the dominating consideration in the design of the letters. In adult writing, the letter b is the most often misread letter.

    2. Uppercase and lowercase letters were kept as similar as possible.

3. PreCursive letters and cursive letters were kept as similar as possible.

4. PreCursive letters were designed so that, with the addition of a cursive joining stroke, the PreCursive becomes the cursive model.

5. Consideration was given to aesthetic design and balance of each letter and to its pleasing appearance in a complete passage of text.

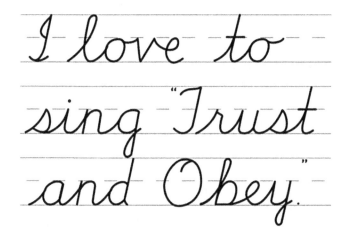

In the fifth and sixth grades, this series also offers several variations of selected uppercase cursive letters. These alternate letters are presented in an effort to renew each student's interest in handwriting and to guide students as they develop individualized handwriting that is both attractive and legible.

Stroke formations

The PreCursive alphabet

A
(1) Drop left.
(2) Drop right.
(3) Cross.

a
Begin at one,
Swing around to lock,
Retrace and curve.

B
Drop,
Retrace and swing
  around to lock,
Retrace and swing
  around to lock.

b
Drop,
Retrace and swing
  around to lock.

C
Begin at one,
Swing around to five.

c
Begin at one,
Swing around to five.

D
Drop,
Swing around and up
  to lock.

d
Begin at one,
Swing around and up,
Climb high,
Retrace and curve.

E
Begin at one,
Swerve around toward
  three,
Swing around to five.

e
Swing up toward one
  and around to five.

F
(1) Drop.
(2) Glide right.
(3) Glide right.

f
(1) Begin at one,
    Swing around and
    drop low.
(2) Cross.

G
(1) Begin at one,
    Swing around to three
    and drop.
(2) Cross.

g
Begin at one,
Swing around to lock,
Drop low and hook.

H
(1) Drop.
(2) Drop.
(3) Cross.

h
Drop,
Retrace and swing
  right,
Drop and curve.

I
(1) Drop.
(2) Cross.
(3) Cross.

i
Drop and curve.
Dot.

J — Drop and hook.

K — (1) Drop.
(2) Drop left,
    Then right and curve.

L — Drop.
Glide right.

m — Drop, retrace and swing
    right,
Drop, retrace and swing
    right,
Drop and curve.

n — Drop, retrace and swing
    right,
Drop and curve.

O — Begin at one,
Swing around to lock.

P — Drop,
Retrace and swing
    around to lock.

Q — (1) Begin at one,
    Swing around to lock.
(2) Slash and curve.

R — Drop,
Retrace and swing
    around to lock,
Drop right and curve.

j — Drop low and hook.
Dot.

k — (1) Drop.
(2) Drop left,
    Then right and curve.

l — Drop and curve.

m — Drop, retrace and swing
    right,
Drop, retrace and swing
    right,
Drop and curve.

n — Drop, retrace and swing
    right,
Drop and curve.

o — Begin at one,
Swing around to lock.

p — Drop low,
Retrace and swing
    around to lock.

q — Begin at one,
Swing around to lock,
Drop low and crook.

r — Drop,
Retrace and swing
    right.

S	Begin at one, Swerve around and back, Stop at seven.
T	(1) Drop. (2) Cross.
U	Drop and swing up, Retrace and curve.
V	Drop right, Climb right.
W	Drop and swing up, Retrace and swing up.
X	(1) Drop right and curve. (2) Drop left.
y	Drop and swing up, Retrace, Drop and hook.
Z	Glide right, Drop left, Glide right.
s	Begin at one, Swerve around and back, Stop at seven.
t	(1) Drop and curve. (2) Cross.
u	Drop and swing up, Retrace and curve.
v	Drop right, Climb right.
w	Drop and swing up, Retrace and swing up.
x	(1) Drop right and curve. (2) Drop left.
y	Drop and swing up, Retrace, Drop low and hook.
z	Glide right, Drop left, Glide right.

The Cursive alphabet

Begin at one,
Swing around to lock,
Retrace and curve.

Swing up and drop,
Retrace and swing
around to lock,
Retrace and swing
around to lock,
Sweep out.

Begin at one,
Swing around to five.

Drop and loop left,
Swing around and over
to lock.

Begin at one,
Swing around toward
three,
Swing around to five.

(1) Swing over and up,
Drop and swing left.
(2) Cross.

Begin at one,
Swing around to three,
Drop low and loop.

(1) Swing up and drop.
(2) Drop and climb left,
Then glide right.

Swing around and up,
Drop and swing left,
Retrace and sweep up.

Swing up and around
to one,
Retrace and swing
around to lock,
Retrace and curve.

Swing up,
Curve left and drop,
Retrace and swing
around to lock,
Sweep out.

Swing up and around
to one,
Retrace and swing
around to five.

Swing up and around
to one,
Retrace and swing
around and up,
Climb high,
Retrace and curve.

Swing up toward one
and around to five.

Swing up,
Curve left and drop low,
Curve right and up to lock,
Bounce.

Swing up and around
to one,
Retrace and swing
around to lock,
Drop low and loop.

Swing up,
Curve left and drop,
Retrace and swing right,
Drop and curve.

Swing up,
Drop and curve.
Dot.

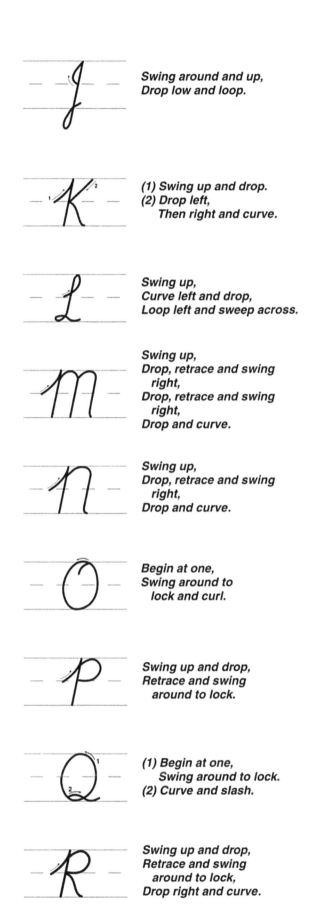

Swing around and up,
Drop low and loop.

(1) Swing up and drop.
(2) Drop left,
      Then right and curve.

Swing up,
Curve left and drop,
Loop left and sweep across.

Swing up,
Drop, retrace and swing
   right,
Drop, retrace and swing
   right,
Drop and curve.

Swing up,
Drop, retrace and swing
   right,
Drop and curve.

Begin at one,
Swing around to
   lock and curl.

Swing up and drop,
Retrace and swing
   around to lock.

(1) Begin at one,
      Swing around to lock.
(2) Curve and slash.

Swing up and drop,
Retrace and swing
   around to lock,
Drop right and curve.

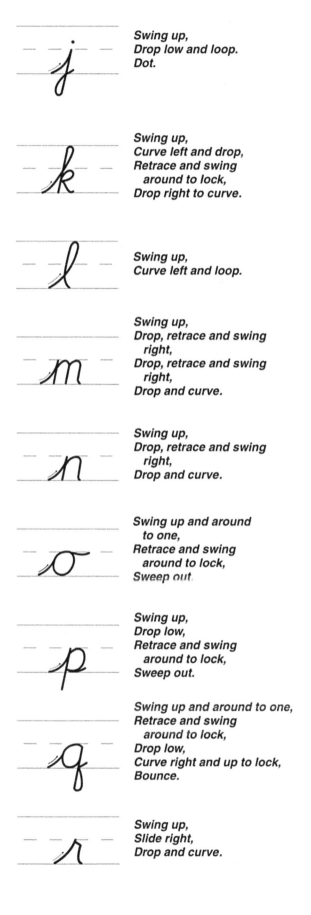

Swing up,
Drop low and loop.
Dot.

Swing up,
Curve left and drop,
Retrace and swing
   around to lock,
Drop right to curve.

Swing up,
Curve left and loop.

Swing up,
Drop, retrace and swing
   right,
Drop, retrace and swing
   right,
Drop and curve.

Swing up,
Drop, retrace and swing
   right,
Drop and curve.

Swing up and around
   to one,
Retrace and swing
   around to lock,
Sweep out.

Swing up,
Drop low,
Retrace and swing
   around to lock,
Sweep out.

Swing up and around to one,
Retrace and swing
   around to lock,
Drop low,
Curve right and up to lock,
Bounce.

Swing up,
Slide right,
Drop and curve.

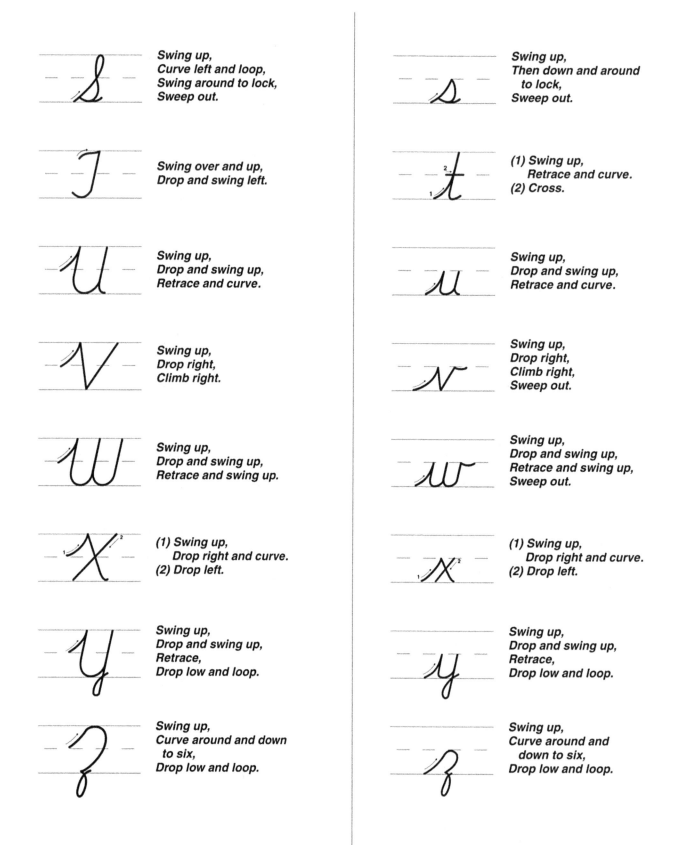

Swing up,
Curve left and loop,
Swing around to lock,
Sweep out.

Swing over and up,
Drop and swing left.

Swing up,
Drop and swing up,
Retrace and curve.

Swing up,
Drop right,
Climb right.

Swing up,
Drop and swing up,
Retrace and swing up.

(1) Swing up,
    Drop right and curve.
(2) Drop left.

Swing up,
Drop and swing up,
Retrace,
Drop low and loop.

Swing up,
Curve around and down
  to six,
Drop low and loop.

Swing up,
Then down and around
  to lock,
Sweep out.

(1) Swing up,
    Retrace and curve.
(2) Cross.

Swing up,
Drop and swing up,
Retrace and curve.

Swing up,
Drop right,
Climb right,
Sweep out.

Swing up,
Drop and swing up,
Retrace and swing up,
Sweep out.

(1) Swing up,
    Drop right and curve.
(2) Drop left.

Swing up,
Drop and swing up,
Retrace,
Drop low and loop.

Swing up,
Curve around and
  down to six,
Drop low and loop.

The numerals

0   Begin at one,
Swing around to lock.

1   Drop.

2   Begin at eleven,
Swing right and down
to the left,
Glide right.

3   Begin at eleven,
Swing around toward nine,
Swing around to seven.

4   (1) Drop and glide right.
(2) Drop.

5   (1) Drop and swing
around to seven.
(2) Glide right.

6   Swing down and around
to lock.

7   Glide right,
Drop left.

8   Begin at one,
Swerve around and back,
Then up and around to lock.

9   Begin at one,
Swing around to lock,
Drop.

Teaching handwriting

Teacher attitudes

As you teach handwriting, your own handwriting provides a model for your students. Your handwriting must reinforce what you teach. Whether you make charts, write on the chalkboard, or compose personal notes to the students, you should write in the PreCursive or cursive writing style. Your attitude of working to improve your own handwriting will make your students more willing to work to develop theirs.

Seating arrangements

For any instruction in handwriting, seating arrangements should make the best use of lighting so that students have no shadows on their papers. Overhead lighting should fill in most shadows and provide even illumination in all parts of the room. In addition, natural light should come at an angle so that a student's writing hand will not cast shadows on his paper. Thus, for the right-handed student, natural light should come over his left shoulder; for the left-handed student, natural light should come over his right shoulder.

If you seat students by groups to make the best use of lighting, you will notice other advantages as well. Seating left-handed students together prevents writing arm collision. In addition, when you give special instructions to left-handed students, you can give them to all left-handed students at once.

Desk position and posture

Good posture affects handwriting. Each child should sit comfortably in his chair with his feet on the floor. The desk should be slightly higher than the student's waist. The student should sit, not leaning to the left or to the right, but bending slightly forward. His forearms should rest on his desk.

Paper position

The position of the paper is related to the child's posture. Each student should place his paper directly in front of his eyes and under his writing hand. The nonwriting hand lies on the paper to hold it still. The slant of the paper will allow him to see around his hand as he works; thus he will not have to lean to the left or right to see his work. A right-handed student will tilt his paper to the left so that it lies parallel to his writing arm. The left-handed student will tilt his paper to the right 30 to 45 degrees. These paper positions will eliminate the hooked-hand position which restricts hand and finger movement needed for writing. The hooked-hand position must also be avoided to prevent poor posture.

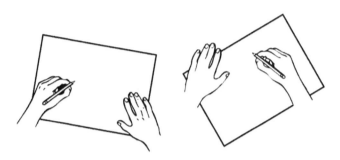

Pencil hold

In the accepted position for pencil hold, the thumb and the index finger grasp the pencil, letting it rest on the middle finger. The last two fingers arch under the middle finger to support it. The hand rests on its side. The student should hold the pencil about one inch from the writing point. The pencil will point toward the shoulder. A student should hold his pencil lightly enough so that you can pull it out of his hand with little resistance. In general, low or medium pressure produces better writing. Teaching correct pencil hold is one of your greatest responsibilities as a primary teacher. It is very difficult and often impossible to try to correct an improper pencil hold that is an established habit.

Handwriting paper

In the Beginnings program and continuing through grade 2, handwriting paper with half-inch lines is used for all handwriting activities. This paper is available from BJU Press, or you may make copies of Appendix page A7.

Writing at the chalkboard

Writing at the chalkboard provides the student the opportunity to practice letter formations under the watchful eye of the teacher. The activity also allows for the development of the large muscles which are used in the writing process.

The following guidelines should be followed to make chalkboard writing a meaningful activity:

1. The child should stand comfortably about an arm's length from the chalkboard, allowing room for the elbow to bend at the proper angle (down and away from the body). Both feet should be on the floor.
2. All writing should be done at the student's eye level.
3. The chalk should be held between the thumb and the first two fingers. It should be long enough to be easily held.
4. The writing should be done with light, sweeping strokes, with the end of the chalk rounded so that it will not squeak.

Special handwriting problems

Illegible handwriting is often a clue to both you and the parents that a child may have special learning problems. Some children cannot write well because they are not mature enough to acquire the motor skills that are necessary to form letters and words. Other children may have poor vision, a problem that a visit to an optometrist will often solve. A small number of children have a specific learning disability that makes it difficult for them to remember the vast amounts of information they are exposed to each day. Students with learning problems should be referred to a learning specialist for evaluation and diagnosis.

The simplified letter forms of the PreCursive alphabet can be of great help to children with learning disabilities. Making the transition to cursive writing puts an end to most reversal problems. The child with a learning disability can often achieve greater legibility in writing the PreCursive and cursive letter forms.

Teacher letter formation

Students can easily master letter formations if you follow the procedure listed below:

1. Verbalize the letter formation as you write each new letter on the chalkboard. If a letter has more than one stroke, use a different color of chalk for each stroke.
2. Have students stand and air-trace the letter with you as you verbalize the letter formation again.
3. Direct students in small groups to write the letter on the chalkboard as you verbalize the letter formation once more.
4. Guide activities on the worktext page. Point out to the students the arrow that gives the stroke direction, finger-trace the gray letter, and then pencil-trace the dotted model.
5. Circulate among the students as they practice the new letters. Make sure they are writing each letter correctly. Evaluation of the finished letters may not reveal incorrect stroke direction; however, when students increase their writing speed, these incorrect strokes will lead to illegible writing.

Letter alignment

Uneven or illegible writing is often the result of letters that do not rest on the baseline. Improper letter height can also produce an uneven top alignment. The simplicity of letter forms used in this series helps each student maintain proper letter alignment. Most letters are given a specific starting point related to one of several guidelines.

top line ——————————

midline — — — —

baseline ——————————

Slant of letters

One of the major causes of illegibility is irregular letter slant. Children often experience their greatest difficulty with slant during the transition to cursive writing. The PreCursive alphabet avoids this transition problem by presenting slanted letters from the beginning. Although an approximate slant of 5 to 15 degrees is suggested, the emphasis should always be on consistency without extremes.

Spacing

Even spacing between letters and words is essential to legible writing. Carefully designed worktext activities guide each student in developing the correct spacing. The shaded areas on the writing lines teach students proper word spacing.

Students need to know how to leave margins and how to correctly place their writing on the paper. The special forms needed for writing correspondence, addressing envelopes, and composing poetry are all part of the handwriting instruction given in *HANDWRITING for Christian Schools*.

1. Do I hold my pencil correctly?
2. Do I have good posture?
3. Are all my letters resting on the baseline?
4. Do all small letters touch the midline, and do all tall letters touch the top line?
5. Are the spaces between the letters and words even?
6. Do all my letters slant the same way?
7. Are all my downstrokes parallel?
8. Are all my letters with loops well formed?
9. Are all closed letters formed correctly?

By comparing past and present work, the students can be encouraged to improve their handwriting. The work can be kept in a writing folder and individual assignments for writing practice can be made from the papers. If this comparison is made on a regular basis, it will keep the students' attention centered on improvement and will help to positively motivate them.

Teacher evaluation

The evaluation form found in the Appendix is designed for your use when you evaluate each student's handwriting. It also provides space for helpful suggestions to students and parents as to how handwriting skills can be improved.

Two pretests are included in the worktext. On these pages students are asked to form letters they have not been taught. These are to help you note the letters that are going to require the most attention. They also provide a basis for information to help each student see his growth. Obviously these pages should not be graded or sent home.

The assessment pages included throughout the book should indicate progress made by the student. These pages, when compared by the students to pretests and past assessments, will show them their progress and encourage them to continue improving. These pages may be graded but should be kept for evaluating progress during the entire year. Two posttests, one following the PreCursive section of the book and the other following the cursive section, should give you an accurate picture of the students' learning. Compare these pretests and past assessments to the students' present achievement.

The following questions may serve as a guide for evaluating handwriting. (See the evaluation sheet, Appendix page A19.)

1. Posture
   Is the child sitting correctly?
   Is he facing his desk?
   Are his forearm and writing hand resting on the desk?
2. Paper position
   Is the paper placed to allow the student to see his writing as he writes?
3. Pencil hold

Neatness

Neatness also contributes to legibility. You may want to teach the children to eliminate undesirable handwriting by drawing one line through it rather than scribbling over or erasing it. Sometimes their vigorous erasing eliminates both the writing and the paper. Of course, learning to erase small mistakes properly comes from instruction in handwriting also. Teach students to think about what they are writing to avoid careless errors, but be realistic about the degree of neatness you expect from them.

Rhythm

Rhythm is the regularity of pressure patterns of fingers on the writing instrument. When we write, we tend to put more pressure on the instrument as we draw the line down toward us and less pressure as we push it up and away. Because of the simple one-stroke letters, students begin to learn rhythm from the outset of instruction in PreCursive. It will become a part of the student's writing when he begins to see whole words, when he attains a speed that is appropriate for his skill, and when he eliminates unnecessary tension from his pencil hold and small muscle movements. Students need to attain consistency of rhythm before they work to increase their speed.

Evaluation of handwriting

Student evaluation

In order to be most effective, the evaluation of handwriting should directly involve the student. HANDWRITING for Christian Schools recognizes the importance of teaching the students to evaluate their own progress.

A classroom checklist that is displayed where it can be seen at all times will help each student correct errors in his writing as they occur. It should include the following questions:

Is there slight tension in the hand? (Watch for collapsed first finger joint or white finger tips.)

Are the first finger and the thumb crossed?

Is the pencil pointed toward the shoulder?

4. Letter formation

Are letters formed according to the model or handwriting chart?

5. Letter alignment

Do letters rest approximately on the baseline?

Do ascenders ascend to the proper point?

Do descenders descend to the proper point?

6. Slant of letters

Is the slant consistent?

Is it too extreme, causing legibility problems? (If necessary, allow left-handed writers to write vertically or slightly backhanded.)

Is the slant between 5 and 15 degrees to the right?

7. Spacing

Is the spacing fairly even?

Is the spacing wide enough to keep letters from running together?

Are individual words spaced closely enough to facilitate reading but far enough to keep words distinguishable?

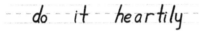

8. Rhythm and flow

Does the rhythm provide consistent letter formation?

9. Neatness

What is the overall appearance of the paper?

As in other subjects that you teach, you will correct common handwriting errors in front of the entire class. Errors that occur in the handwriting of only a few students you can correct as you walk around the classroom while the students are writing. In either case, keep your words of criticism and of praise specific. Remember that handwriting is a skill that, like every other skill, demands practice to master. Consequently, your criticism must concentrate on a small enough area so that the student can grasp the problem and correct it.

Remember, the purpose of teaching handwriting is to help the student achieve legibility and neatness and to make handwriting enjoyable instead of a dreaded experience. The purpose is not to make every student's handwriting look like every other student's handwriting. If the students are to enjoy the handwriting time, they must feel relaxed and successful.

Developing handwriting consciousness

Displaying students' handwriting

Students' work should be displayed whenever possible, omitting no student in this effective method of approval. Several bulletin board displays are included on Appendix pages 3-6. Used throughout the year, they will instill a sense of pride in each student, encouraging him to improve his handwriting and to do it heartily as unto the Lord.

Other classroom activities using handwriting

When the students do other activities that use writing, have them use the same lined paper or lines of the same size as those used for handwriting activities. To label maps and drawings or other projects, cut out pieces of lined paper and glue them down. For all activities involving handwriting, consider the length of the activity. Choose assignments that your students can write comfortably in a reasonable amount of time. Even though the primary goal of an activity may be something other than good handwriting, students must understand that all writing contributes to writing habits, and thus, every activity involving writing is also a handwriting exercise.

Objectives

Given the proper instruction the students will be able to do the following:

Match each letter to its uppercase or lowercase counterpart and to its PreCursive or cursive counterpart.

Arrange letters in proper alphabetical sequence. Use numerals.

Write legibly, incorporating neatness, consistent slant, consistent spacing, and correct alignment.

Demonstrate good posture, correct paper position, and proper tension-free pencil hold.

Write the PreCursive alphabet letters.

Use adequate spacing between PreCursive letters, words, and sentences.

Arrange work neatly on paper.

Use vocabulary that describes letter spacing: space, dashes, indent.

Use vocabulary that describes letter alignment: top line, midline, baseline.

Demonstrate appropriate size and correct alignment of letters on lined paper.

Demonstrate correct slant in both PreCursive and cursive writing.

Write in both PreCursive and cursive with rhythm and speed.

Read cursive writing.

Point out the PreCursive letter visible in each cursive letter model.

Write the cursive letters.

Use joining strokes in cursive writing.

Materials and Preparation

Have available:

- Handwriting charts.
- A copy of the Timothy Time puppet (Appendix, p. A9).

Prepare:

- The Timothy Time puppet.
- A PreCursive model of each student's name on the front of each worktext.
- A tape recording of "The Handwriting Song" found on Appendix page A21.
- A copy of "The Handwriting Song" on a transparency or chart paper.

———— Lesson Content ————

Introduction

Introduce the student worktexts and the character Timothy Time—Let Timothy pretend to assist with the distribution of the worktexts.

> Timothy Time, a boy from Switzerland, knows how to write each PreCursive letter. He will show you how to make many of the letters. He often uses a clock from his uncle's clock shop to tell the time at which a PreCursive letter begins. Most PreCursive letters begin at twelve o'clock or one o'clock. Timothy Time knows a lot about writing and clocks.

Generate interest in the worktext by asking the following questions about the cover:

- ➤ Who is the boy on the cover?
- ➤ What is he doing?
- ➤ What kind of clock is on the cover?
- ➤ What kind of letters are shown on the cover?

Tell the students that after they have practiced the PreCursive alphabet for a while, they will be learning the cursive alphabet.

Lead a discussion about proper book care—Allow time for students to look at their worktexts. Discuss the following points:

1. Always handle the worktext with clean hands.
2. Hold the worktext properly and turn the pages carefully.
3. Never write or mark in the worktext until told to do so.
4. Remove pages only when told to do so.

Tell the students that you will frequently check to see if they are taking good care of their worktexts.

After every ten lessons or so, you may want to draw a star on the inside cover of each worktext that is kept neat.

Teach "The Handwriting Song"—Direct the students to "The Handwriting Song." Ask a volunteer to read the first stanza of the song. Allow the children to listen to the tape recording of the music. Let Timothy Time pretend to assist you as you lead the class in singing the song.

Skill Development

Introduce the handwriting charts—Lead the class in saying the name of each PreCursive letter on the handwriting charts. Point out that for many of the letters the only difference between the uppercase and lowercase letter is the size. Tell the students that when writing they will frequently refer to the models on the charts.

You will want to be sure to send home to parents the letter on worktext page 95.

Optional Activity

Lead the students in a tracking activity—Use Appendix page A11 to prepare a tracking activity. Instruct the students to track horizontally and vertically as they follow a path to school. Additional tracking activities can be done on the chalkboard or on construction paper.

Lesson 2　　　　**The Clock Maker's Shop**　　　　**Worktext page 3**

Materials and Preparation

Have available:

- The Timothy Time puppet.
- The tape recording of "The Handwriting Song."

——— Lesson Content ———

Introduction

Create interest in today's lesson—Let Timothy Time pretend to sing "The Handwriting Song" on the back of the student worktext. Allow a student to hold Timothy Time as the class sings the songs. Use the recording as needed.

Skill Development

Guide a discussion of illustrations—Use the illustrations on the inside cover of the student worktext to show correct posture, paper position, and pencil hold.

Demonstrate handwriting posture—Tell the students to bend slightly forward, not leaning to the left or to the right, with forearms resting on the desk. Check to see that they are sitting comfortably in their chairs with both feet on the floor. Be sure each desk is slightly higher than the student's waist. Make notes about desk height problems so that seating assignments can be changed or mechanical adjustments made.

Demonstrate paper position—The student's paper should be positioned at a slant that approximately parallels the slant of his writing arm.

Demonstrate pencil hold—Tell each student to grasp his pencil lightly about an inch from the point. Use the following jingle to teach the children how to hold a pencil:

> Three Finger Men hold the pencil in place.
> Pointer and Thumbkin on top, face to face.
> Tall Man likes pencil to rest on his side,
> And two Lazy Men go along for the ride.

Guided Practice

Guide the completion of worktext page 3—Allow a volunteer to read the title of the page and the instructions. Ask the students what they notice about the letters on the clocks on the page. *(They are the lowercase PreCursive letters.)* Instruct the students to underline each letter that begins at one o'clock as they follow the path to the clock maker.

Conclude the lesson by leading the students in singing "The Handwriting Song" again.

Optional Activity

Direct an activity to strengthen muscle coordination—Allow the students to use modeling dough to form a clock and numbers to tell the time.

Modeling Dough Recipe

> 2 c. flour
> 1 c. salt
>
> Moisten with water (approximately 1 c.).
> Add food coloring or tempera powder.
> Store in an airtight container.

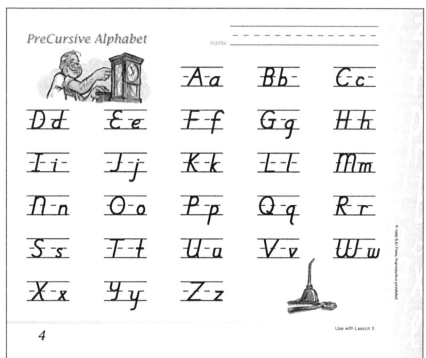

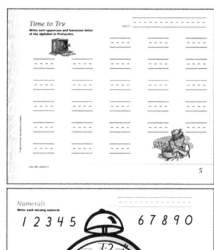

Materials and Preparation

Have available:
- The tape recording of "The Handwriting Song."

Prepare:
- A PreCursive name model for each student's desk.

———— Lesson Content ————

Introduction

Lead the class in singing "The Handwriting Song"—Divide the class into two groups. Instruct one group to sing the first verse while the second group pantomimes the words. Then have the other group sing the second verse of the song. Use the recording as needed.

Pretest

Guide the completion of the PreCursive pretest on worktext page 5—Call attention to the PreCursive name models attached to the students' desks. Instruct them to use the model as a guide as they neatly write their names on page 5. Allow a volunteer to read the page title and the instructions. Point out to the students that they are going to try to write the letters of the alphabet in PreCursive as Timothy Time tries to construct a clock in his uncle's clock shop. Tell them to use the models on page 4 as a guide. Let the Timothy Time puppet assist you as you walk around the room and remind students of good posture, paper position, and pencil hold. Encourage the students to attempt each letter but not to spend a long time on each one (about 30 seconds on a given letter). Stress that the page will not be graded or sent home

but that it will be saved for them to see their progress as they learn the correct way to form each letter.

Direct the completion of the numeral pretest on worktext page 6—Allow a student to read the instructions and then instruct the class to complete the page by adding the numerals to the clock. After the activity has been completed, direct a student to read the time on the clock.

Collect the papers and then make and record pertinent observations such as those listed below:

➤ Which letters are the most difficult for students to write and may require more than one lesson to teach?
➤ Which students have problems with reversals?
➤ Which students need additional activities at school and at home to strengthen fine muscle coordination?
➤ Which students have no concept of alignment and spacing?

Collect each student's pretest so that you can periodically refer to it to note progress.

Optional Activity

Direct the students in a tracking activity—Use Appendix, page A13 to make a tracking activity.

> This tracking activity may be difficult for some students. Encourage them to do their best and reassure them that it is simply practice.

Materials and Preparation

Have available:

- A model of a clock.
- The Timothy Time puppet.
- Handwriting charts.

Prepare:

- Handwriting lines on the chalkboard.

——— Lesson Content ———

Introduction

Create interest in today's lesson—Lead the class in singing "The Handwriting Song." Have the Timothy Time puppet compliment the class for singing well.

Vocabulary Development

Introduce terms to describe letter alignment and spacing—Direct the students' attention to the lines on the chalkboard. Label according to the illustration below.

top line — — — — —

midline — — — —

baseline ———————

Use the word *space* to refer to the distance between letters written individually or between words.

A space equals the distance of two dashes of the midline in the worktext. On most handwriting paper you will need to make an appropriate comparison.

Skill Development

Demonstrate the formation of uppercase and lowercase *c* and *o*—Direct the students' attention to the handwriting charts. Have Timothy Time read the jingle:

> Our first letter starts at one.
> Can you guess it just for fun?

Verbalize the direction of the stroke as you first finger-trace the letter *c* on the clock and then write it on the chalkboard. Point out that the only difference between uppercase and lowercase *c* is the size. Instruct the class to air-trace both letters. Follow the same procedure for letter *o*.

C   *Begin at one,*
     Swing around to five.

c   *Begin at one,*
     Swing around to five.

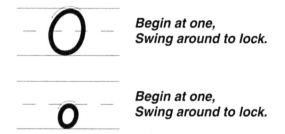

Begin at one,
Swing around to lock.

Begin at one,
Swing around to lock.

Guided Practice

Guide the completion of worktext page 7—Let a volunteer read Ecclesiastes 3:1. Explain that this verse tells that the Lord orders our time and that we should spend our time wisely by serving the Lord, because our time really belongs to Him.

Discuss the picture of the sundial—Explain to the class that the sundial was one of the earliest ways man had of telling time. The shadow the sun casts on the dial provides a very accurate way of telling time. The face of a sundial is much like the face of a clock. Lead a discussion about what it would be like to use sundials if we had no clocks. Encourage the students to trace the PreCursive *c* on the sundial.

Direct the completion of the handwriting activity—Point out that the shaded area indicates the amount of space that should be left between each letter. Instruct the students to follow the procedure listed below before they begin writing letters.

1. Note the arrow that indicates the direction of the stroke.
2. Trace the gray letter with your finger.
3. Pencil-trace the dotted lines.

Circulate among the students and make sure they form each letter correctly. Encourage them to do their work gladly as unto the Lord.

Optional Activity

Direct an art activity—Allow the students to fingerpaint the PreCursive letters *c* and *o*.

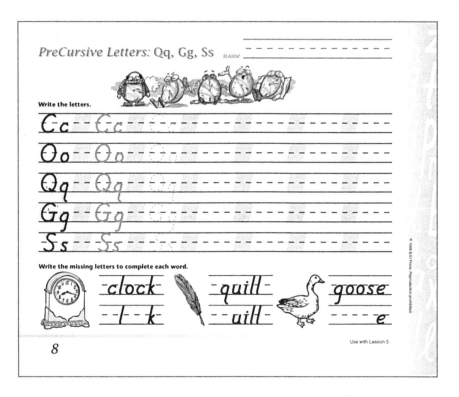

Materials and Preparation

Have available:

- The Timothy Time puppet.
- Colored chalk.

———— Lesson Content ————

Introduction

Review the handwriting techniques—Use the Timothy Time puppet to direct the students in a review of good writing posture, paper position, and pencil hold. Sing "The Handwriting Song."

Skill Development

Review the formation of uppercase and lowercase *c* and *o*—Point to the letters on the handwriting charts and verbalize each stroke.

> See Lesson 4 for verbalization of strokes.

Demonstrate the formation of uppercase and lowercase *q, g,* and *s*—Verbalize the direction of the strokes as you write each letter on the chalkboard. Use different colors of chalk for each new stroke. Direct the class to air-trace the uppercase and lowercase letters.

(1) Begin at one,
*   Swing around to lock.*
(2) Slash and curve.

Begin at one,
Swing around to lock,
Drop low and crook.

(1) Begin at one,
*   Swing around to three*
*   and drop.*
(2) Cross.

Begin at one,
Swing around to lock,
Drop low and hook.

Begin at one,
Swerve around and
* back,*
Stop at seven.

Begin at one,
Swerve around and
* back,*
Stop at seven.

Guided Practice

Guide the completion of worktext page 8—Encourage the students to trace the letters in the clock illustrations. Ask a volunteer to read the instructions for completing the first activity. Direct the students to first finger-trace the gray letters, then pencil-trace the dotted lines, and finally write the correct letters on the remainder of the line. After the first activity, instruct a student to read the directions for the work at the bottom of the page. Call attention to the space provided for each missing letter before instructing the class to complete the activity.

One dash represents the width of most lower-case letters.

Optional Activity

Direct a writing activity using sand—Tell the students to write the letters *Cc, Oo, Qq, Gg,* and *Ss* in a small amount of sand placed in a shoebox top or tray.

Lesson 6   PreCursive Letters: *Ee, Aa, Dd*   Worktext page 9

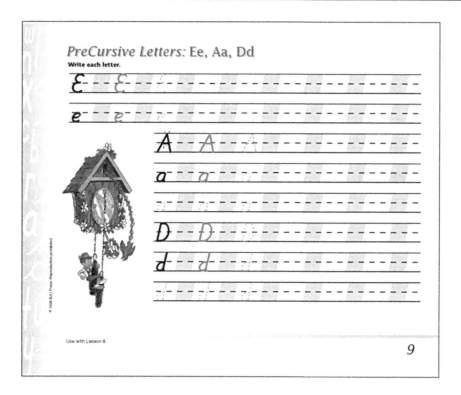

Materials and Preparation

Have available:

- A picture of a cuckoo clock (Appendix, p. A15).
- Colored chalk.

Prepare:

- The poem "The Big Clock" in PreCursive on chart paper.
- Handwriting lines on the chalkboard.

——— Lesson Content ———

Introduction

Generate interest in today's lesson—Read a poem about a clock. Display the picture of the cuckoo clock. Read the following poem to the class and then lead the students as they read it in unison.

The Big Clock

Slowly ticks the big clock;
Tick-tock, tick-tock!
But cuckoo clock ticks double-quick;
Tick-a-tock-a, Tick-a-tock-a,
Tick-a-tock-a, tick!

Skill Development

Demonstrate the formation of uppercase and lowercase *e*—Verbalize the direction of each stroke as you finger-trace the letter on the cuckoo clock and then write the letter on the chalkboard. Point out the one o'clock start of uppercase *e* and the nine o'clock start of lowercase *e*.

 *Begin at one,*
Swerve around toward
three,
Swing around to five.

 *Swing up toward one*
and around to five.

 The serif is the slight curve that is formed at the end of the stroke. Tell the students to demonstrate the serif by standing on their tiptoes. The curve formed by their toes is a good example of the serif.

Demonstrate the formation of uppercase and lowercase *a* and *d*—Verbalize the direction of the strokes as you write each letter on the chalkboard. Use different colors of chalk for each stroke. Point out that the lowercase forms of these letters begin at one o'clock and end in a serif.

 *(1) Drop left.*
(2) Drop right.
(3) Cross.

 *Begin at one,*
Swing around to lock,
Retrace and curve.

Guided Practice

Guide the completion of worktext page 9—Direct the students' attention to the cuckoo clock and ask them to try to find the hidden letter. *(The hidden letter is the uppercase* a *that forms the roof of the clock.)* Remind them that uppercase *a* will begin at twelve o'clock.

Instruct the students to read the instructions and complete the activity—Remind them to finger-trace the gray letters, then pencil-trace the dotted lines, and finally write the letters on the remainder of the line.

 *Drop,*
Swing around and up
to lock.

 *Begin at one,*
Swing around and up,
Climb high,
Retrace and curve.

Optional Activity

Direct an art activity—Tell the students to draw a cuckoo clock on construction paper. Instruct them to hide the Pre-Cursive letters *a* and *d* in their clocks and then have a neighbor search for the hidden letters.

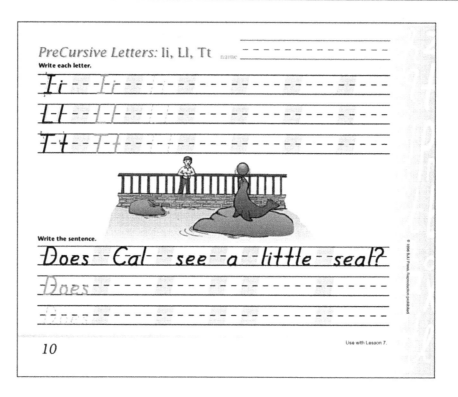

PreCursive Letters: Ii, Ll, Tt　name

Write each letter.

Ii

Ll

Tt

Write the sentence.

Does Cal see a little seal?

Does

10

Use with Lesson 7.

Materials and Preparation

Have available:

- The model of a clock.
- The Timothy Time puppet.
- Colored chalk.

Prepare:

- Handwriting lines on the chalkboard.

——— Lesson Content ———

Introduction

Review handwriting techniques—Use the Timothy Time puppet to review posture, paper position, and pencil hold. Have him lead "The Handwriting Song." Also use the puppet as you talk about the correct care of the worktext.

> Remind the students of the star award that will be given to those who keep their worktexts neat and clean.

Skill Development

Demonstrate the formation of uppercase and lowercase *i, l,* and *t*—Use the clock model to show that *i* is a twelve o'clock letter. Verbalize the directions of the strokes as you write each letter on the chalkboard. Use different colors of chalk as you demonstrate each stroke. Direct the class in air-tracing the uppercase and lowercase *i*. Follow the same procedure for *l* and *t*. Pay careful attention to the serifs on the lowercase letters.

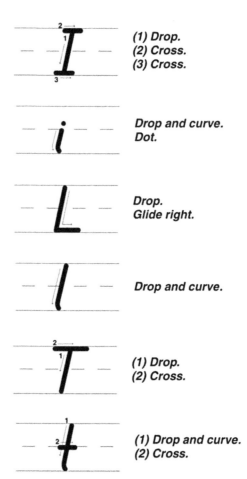

(1) Drop.
(2) Cross.
(3) Cross.

Drop and curve.
Dot.

Drop.
Glide right.

Drop and curve.

(1) Drop.
(2) Cross.

(1) Drop and curve.
(2) Cross.

Guided Practice

Guide the completion of worktext page 10—Allow a volunteer to read the instructions for both activities on this page. Ask a student to read the sentence under the picture and answer the question. Remind the students that every sentence begins with an uppercase letter and ends with a punctuation mark. Before students begin the first activity, remind them to note the arrows, trace the dotted lines, and then write the letters in the spaces between the shaded areas of the remainder of the line. Point out that when writing words they are to leave two dashes between each word.

Use the Timothy Time puppet to read the following jingle:

> Space between each word just so,
> And it will look MAGNIFICO!

Optional Activity

Direct composing of words—Write the letters *c, o, q, g, s, a, d, i, l,* and *t* on the chalkboard. Instruct the students to compose as many words as possible from these letters. Tell them to write the words on handwriting paper.

Lesson 8   A Calendar   Worktext page 11

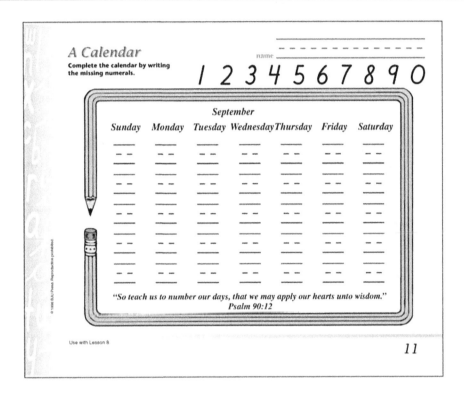

Materials and Preparation

Prepare:

• A classroom calendar for the month of September or a printed calendar that is large enough for the class to read.

——— Lesson Content ———

Introduction

Read the following Mother Goose rhyme.

> Thirty days hath September,
> April, June, and November.
> February has twenty-eight alone;
> All the rest have thirty-one.

Except in leap-year, that's the time
When February's days are twenty-nine.

Direct the students' attention to the classroom calendar—Point out that the basic units of a calendar are day, week, month, and year. Show how numerals tell us the day of the month. Explain that calendars often supply additional information such as holidays, historical dates, and astronomical data such as sunset time, sunrise time, and eclipses.

Skill Development

Introduce the numerals—Ask the students to give the name of the present month *(September)* and the number of days in the month *(30)*. Ask a child to name the numerals that are used on the calendar. Write the numerals *0-9* on the chalkboard, verbalizing each stroke as you write.

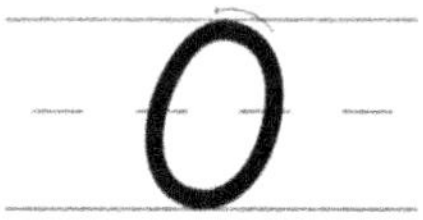

0   *Begin at one,*
Swing around to lock.

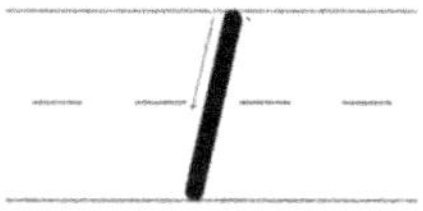

1   *Drop.*

2   *Begin at eleven,*
Swing right and down
  to the left,
Glide right.

3   *Begin at eleven,*
Swing around toward nine,
Swing around to seven.

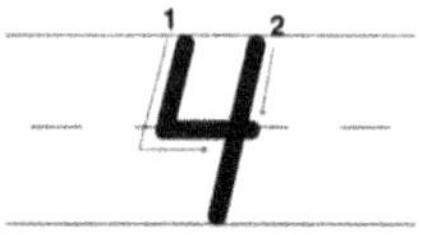

4   *(1) Drop and glide right.*
(2) Drop.

5   *(1) Drop and swing*
    around to seven.
(2) Glide right.

6   *Swing down and around*
  to lock.

7   *Glide right,*
Drop left.

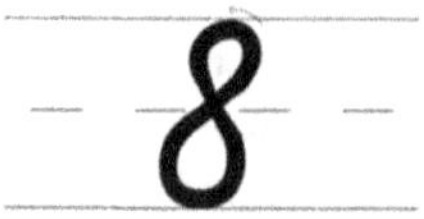

8   *Begin at one,*
Swerve around and back,
Then up and around to lock.

9   *Begin at one,*
Swing around to lock.
Drop.

Guided Practice

Guide the completion of worktext page 11—Read Psalm 90:12 and tell the students that Christians are to be careful not to waste time but to use it wisely for the Lord. Ask what are some wise ways to use time. Write the students' responses on the chalkboard. Ask for a volunteer to read the directions on page 11 and let the students work independently to fill in the calendar. Encourage all the students to be wise time users.

Optional Activity

Direct a numeral writing activity—Help each student to make and illustrate a calendar for the month of his birthday on construction paper. Encourage each to include pictures to show any holidays that occur during that month.

PreCursive Letters: Hh, Kk, Xx   name _____

Write each letter.

Hh -- Hh -- Hh

Kk -- Kk -- Kk

Xx -- Xx -- Xx

eight o'clock   six o'clock   eight o'clock

Write the missing words to complete each sentence.

School begins at eight o'clock

Dinner is at

Bedtime is at

12   Use with Lesson 9.

Materials and Preparation

Have available:

- The model of a clock.
- Colored chalk.

Prepare:

- The following groups of words on sentence strips.

  Time for lunch
  Time for recess
  Time for music
  Time for reading
  Time for dismissal
  Time for chapel

——— Lesson Content ———

Introduction

Generate interest with a clock game—Display the clock and the sentence strips. Choose a volunteer to select a phrase to read and then, using the clock, indicate the time of that activity. Continue the activity until all phrases have been read.

Sing "The Handwriting Song."

Skill Development

Demonstrate the formation of uppercase and lowercase h, k, and x—Verbalize the directions of the strokes as you write the letter *h* on the chalkboard. Use different colors of chalk to demonstrate each stroke. Direct the class in air-

tracing each letter. Continue the same procedure with the letters *k* and *x*.

(1) Drop.
(2) Drop.
(3) Cross.

Drop,
Retrace and swing right,
Drop and curve.

(1) Drop.
(2) Drop left,
Then right and curve.

(1) Drop.
(2) Drop left,
Then right and curve.

(1) Drop right and curve.
(2) Drop left.

(1) Drop right and curve.
(2) Drop left.

Guided Practice

Guide the completion of worktext page 12—Allow a volunteer to read the instructions for both activities. Remind the students to note the shaded area that indicates correct spacing. Call attention to the clocks. Discuss what Timothy Time is doing and then choose volunteers to read the sentences.

Optional Activity

Direct an art activity using construction paper—Write the following groups of words on the board or on chart paper and tell the students to draw clocks to indicate the time they do the activities.

Time for Sunday school
Time for bed
Time for school
Time for church
Time for devotions

Lesson 10　　　　　　A Review

Materials and Preparation

Have available:

- Handwriting paper for each student.
- The Timothy Time puppet.

Prepare:

- Handwriting lines on the chalkboard.

——— Lesson Content ———

Introduction

Review handwriting techniques—Use the Timothy Time puppet to check correct posture, paper position, and pencil hold.

Sing "The Handwriting Song."

Skill Development

Guide a review of one o'clock letters—Verbalize the direction of each stroke as students write lowercase letters *c, o, q, g, s, a,* and *d* on the chalkboard.

Guided Practice

Guide the writing of one o'clock letters—Tell the students to write lowercase letters *c, o, q, g, s, a,* and *d* several times

on their handwriting paper. Remind them to space correctly between the letters.

Initiate a self-evaluation—Distribute the pretest that the students completed in Lesson 3. Direct the students to compare the letters that they wrote today with the letters they wrote on the pretest. Help them note improvements and letters that need more practice. Collect the pretests.

Optional Activity

Direct the writing of hidden words—Write the following letters on the chalkboard or on chart paper. Have the students find the hidden words among the letters and write them on handwriting paper.

i	a	d	g	l	a	d	o	o	c
c	a	l	l	l	a	l	t	c	e
l	i	g	o	o	d	a	q	s	a
q	o	c	g	d	i	c	o	l	d
a	g	d	i	s	e	a	t	o	l

Time to Review

Write each letter and word.

| Cc | Oo | Qq | Gg | Ss | Ee | Aa |

| Dd | Ii | Ll | Tt | Hh | Kk | Xx |

| lad | did | see | the | kid | had | old |

Write the sentence two times.

The lad did a good deed.

Use with Lesson 11.

13

Materials and Preparation

Have available:

- Eleven 3" × 5" cards.
- A paper bag.

Prepare:

- Two clocks on the chalkboard, one set at twelve o'clock and one set at one o'clock.
- Handwriting lines under each clock.
- The index cards with uppercase letters *c, o, q, s, a, d, i, I, t, h,* and *k* and place the cards in a paper bag.

———— Lesson Content ————

Introduction

Sing "The Handwriting Song."

Skill Development

Guide a review of lowercase letters—Choose a student to select a card from the paper bag, name the uppercase letter, and then write its lowercase letter under the clock that shows the time at which the letter begins. After all the lowercase letters have been written, choose a student to draw a line under the letters that have a serif.

Guided Practice

Guide the completion of worktext page 13—Choose a volunteer to read the directions for both activities on this page. Tell another child to read the first part of Proverbs 20:11. Discuss the picture and talk about other good deeds they could do. Remind them to pay close attention to the shaded spaces between letters and words. As they complete the activities on this page, walk around the room and be ready to help any student who has difficulty in writing the sentences.

Optional Activity

Direct a matching activity—Write the letters *C, c, O, o, Q, q, G, g, S, s, E, e, A, a, D, d, I, i, L, l, T,* and *t* on separate 3" × 5" cards. Direct the students to match the uppercase PreCursive letters to the lowercase PreCursive letters.

15

Time for Lunch   name

Write each sentence.

"Take this," the lad said.

"It is a little. It's good."

"All shall eat. See! A little

is a lot. God did it."

14   Use with Lesson 12.

Materials and Preparation

Prepare:

• A bulletin board to display the students' handwriting.

> Worktext page 14 is an assessment page that you may want to remove from the worktext prior to the lesson.

——— Lesson Content ———

Introduction

Review the correct way to hold a pencil—Make sure your students' pencils are soft enough to mark readily and long enough to extend past the first knuckle of the hand. Have Timothy Time say the following jingle:

> If your pencil is too small,
>   Don't you use it—not at all.
> If it is too hard to write,
>   It doesn't matter what its height.
> Get a new one straight and long—
>   It makes writing time a song.

Assessment

Motivate the students for the evaluation on worktext page 14—Discuss the story of the lad with the five loaves and two small fishes (John 6:1-13). Ask for a volunteer to read the story on page 14 before the students write.

Direct the completion of the assessment—Direct the students to write the sentences on page 14. Walk around the room and make sure the students are forming each letter carefully—not too quickly and not too slowly.

After you collect the papers, you will want to compare them with the pretests given in Lesson 2. Note students who are having problems with certain letters and prepare additional practice on handwriting paper.

Evaluate the papers by checking letter formation, letter size, slant of letters, spacing, and alignment. It is important that you make positive comments on each paper. Refer to the introduction for samples of acceptable spacing, slant, and alignment.

Optional Activity

Direct an activity to develop small motor skill coordination—Direct students to twist, bend, and shape chenille wires into the forms of letters they have learned to write.

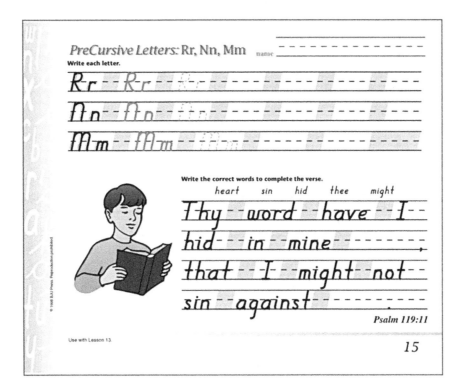

Materials and Preparation

Prepare:

• Handwriting lines on the chalkboard.

────── **Lesson Content** ──────

Introduction

Lead a letter guessing game—Air-trace the letter *r* as you verbalize the stroke. Allow the students to guess the letter you are describing. Continue the same procedure with the letters *n* and *m*.

Skill Development

Demonstrate the formation of uppercase and lowercase *r*, *n*, and *m*—Verbalize the direction of each stroke as you write the letter on the chalkboard. Then tell the students to air-trace each letter.

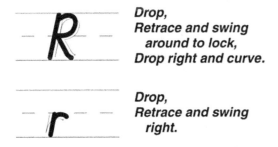

R
Drop,
Retrace and swing
  around to lock,
Drop right and curve.

r
Drop,
Retrace and swing
  right.

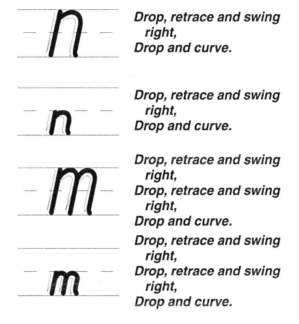

n
Drop, retrace and swing
  right,
Drop and curve.

n
Drop, retrace and swing
  right,
Drop and curve.

m
Drop, retrace and swing
  right,
Drop, retrace and swing
  right,
Drop and curve.

m
Drop, retrace and swing
  right,
Drop, retrace and swing
  right,
Drop and curve.

Guide the writing of words on the chalkboard—Dictate the following words and have students write them on the handwriting lines on the chalkboard.

man	*Nan*	*ram*	*rim*
ran	*mob*	*rob*	*rod*

Guided Practice

Direct the completion of worktext page 15—Direct a student to read the instructions for completing the activities on this page. Choose volunteers to read the sentences and supply the missing words.

Optional Activity

Guide a writing practice—Write the following words and sentences on the chalkboard. Distribute handwriting paper and instruct the students to write the sentences and supply the missing words. Remind them to space correctly between each word.

Words to use:

cone	licked	melt
time	ice cream	

1. I had an ice cream _____ to eat.
2. I _____ a little at a time.
3. It started to _____.
4. I licked a lot at a _____.
5. Soon I ate my _____ cone.

Lesson 14   PreCursive Letters: *Uu, Ww, Yy*   Worktext page 16

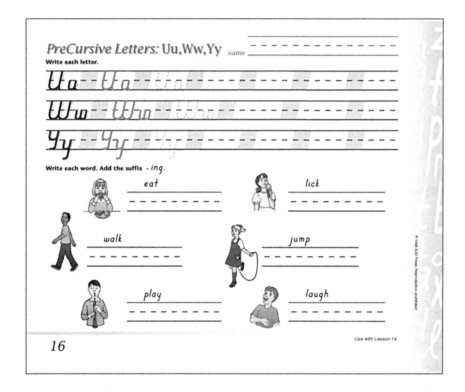

PreCursive Letters: Uu, Ww, Yy   name

Write each letter.

Uu   Uu   Uu

Ww   Ww   Ww

Yy   Yy   Yy

Write each word. Add the suffix *-ing.*

eat

lick

walk

jump

play

laugh

16

Use with Lesson 14

Materials and Preparation

Have available:
- The Timothy Time puppet.
- Handwriting paper for each student.

Prepare:
- Handwriting lines on the chalkboard.
- The following words in PreCursive on the chalkboard.

    play
    find
    buy
    fly

———— Lesson Content ————

Introduction

Motivate the students to write—Use the Timothy Time puppet to lead the class in "The Handwriting Song."

Skill Development

Demonstrate the formation of uppercase and lowercase *u, w,* and *y*—Verbalize the strokes as you write each letter on the chalkboard.

Drop and swing up, Retrace and curve.

18

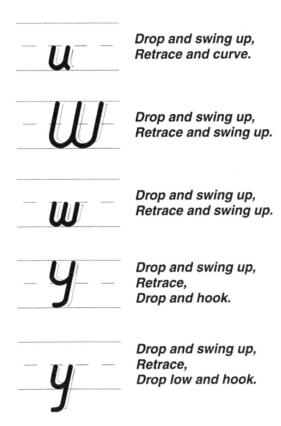

Drop and swing up,
Retrace and curve.

Drop and swing up,
Retrace and swing up.

Drop and swing up,
Retrace and swing up.

Drop and swing up,
Retrace,
Drop and hook.

Drop and swing up,
Retrace,
Drop low and hook.

Discuss the similarities and differences of these letter formations—Ask the students to tell how the letters are alike *(similar rounded strokes)* and how they are different *(u has one rounded stroke, w has two rounded strokes, and y has a short rounded stroke and a long hook)*. Choose volunteers to write the letters on the board as you verbalize each stroke.

Give directions for adding a suffix to a base word—Direct the students' attention to the words written on the chalkboard. Select students to read each word, trace the letters, and add the suffix *-ing*. Remind the students that a suffix is a letter or group of letters that is added to the end of a base word.

Guided Practice

Guide the completion of worktext page 16—Ask a volunteer to read the directions for each activity. Remind the

students to space correctly as they write the letters and words.

Optional Activity

Direct an art activity—Have the students make animal characters using letters that they have learned.

Examples:

Lesson 15   Finding the Base Words

Materials and Preparation

Have available:

- Handwriting paper for each student.

Prepare:

- The following words in PreCursive on the chalkboard.

praying	*opening*
yelling	*hearing*
singing	*raining*
drawing	*painting*
walking	*starting*
camping	*quarrelling*

——— Lesson Content ———

Introduction

Create interest in today's lesson—Direct the students' attention to the first column of words on the chalkboard. Choose five students to pretend to be detectives as they uncover the base words by erasing the suffixes.

Skill Development

Review the formation of the letters that your students do not write correctly—Verbalize the stroke directions as students write the letters on the chalkboard.

Guided Practice

Direct students in writing base words—Direct the students' attention to the second column of words written on the chalkboard. Instruct the students to write the base words on their handwriting paper. After the students have completed the activity, have volunteers use each word in an oral sentence.

Optional Activity

Direct a writing activity—Write the following words on the chalkboard or on chart paper:

eat   snow   count   play   add   hunt

Have the students add the *-ing* suffix to the words. If time permits have the students write sentences using the words with the suffix.

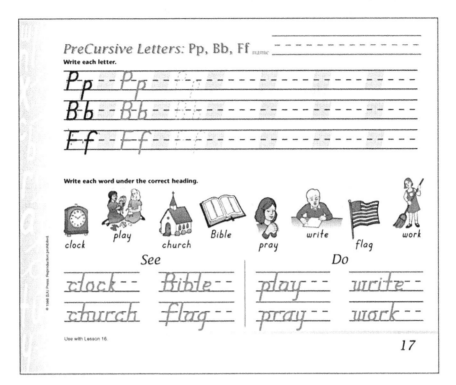

Materials and Preparation

Prepare:

- The following words in PreCursive on the chalkboard.

laugh	*car*	*lion*	*run*
call	*talk*	*hill*	*dog*

- The following headings in PreCursive on the chalkboard with four handwriting lines under each heading.

  See   **Do**

Lesson Content

Introduction

Lead a classifying activity—Choose volunteers to read the headings and words written on the chalkboard. Let students classify the words by writing them under the correct headings. As each word is written, call attention to the letters that have a serif.

Skill Development

Demonstrate the formation of uppercase and lowercase *p*, *b*, and *f*—Verbalize the direction of the strokes as you write each letter on the chalkboard. Point out that lowercase *b* is visible in the uppercase letter and that the lowercase *f* extends below the baseline. Direct the students to air-trace the letters and then practice writing them on the chalkboard.

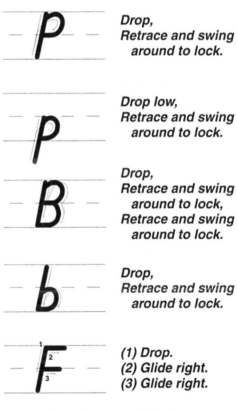

P Drop,
Retrace and swing
around to lock.

p Drop low,
Retrace and swing
around to lock.

B Drop,
Retrace and swing
around to lock,
Retrace and swing
around to lock.

b Drop,
Retrace and swing
around to lock.

F (1) Drop.
(2) Glide right.
(3) Glide right.

f (1) Begin at one,
Swing around and
drop low.
(2) Cross.

Guided Practice

Guide the completion of worktext page 17—Choose a volunteer to read the directions for the activities on this page. Instruct the students to complete the activities independently.

Optional Activity

Direct a classifying activity—Distribute handwriting paper and instruct the students to fold the paper in half and to write "See" on the left side and "Do" on the right side. As you write the following words on the chalkboard, have the students classify them by writing each word under the correct heading. After all the words have been written, have the students illustrate one word from each heading on the back of their papers. (Answers will vary.)

ball	*swim*
numeral	*hike*
kick	*chalk*
desk	*sleep*
goat	*build*
climb	*flower*

Lesson 17   PreCursive Letters: *Jj, Vv, ZZ*   Worktext page 18

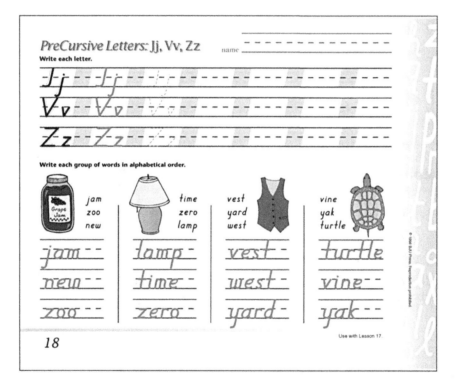

Materials and Preparation

Prepare:

- Handwriting lines on the chalkboard.
- The following words in PreCursive on the chalkboard.

zoom	*zip*	*Zechariah*
vent	*quiet*	*Judges*
jet	*time*	*Psalms*

─────── Lesson Content ───────

Introduction

Create interest in today's lesson—Ask the following questions. Choose volunteers to respond by pointing to the correct letter on the handwriting charts.

1. Which letter comes after *y*?
2. Which letter comes after *u* and before *w*?
3. Which letter comes after *i* and before *k*?
4. Which letter comes after *d* and before *f*?
5. Which letter comes before *h* and after *f*?
6. Which letter comes before *c* and after *a*?
7. Which letter comes before *w* and after *u*?
8. Which letter comes before *s* and after *q*?

Skill Development

**Demonstrate the formation of uppercase and lowercase *j, v,* and *z*—Verbalize the direction of the strokes as you write each letter on the chalkboard. Tell the class to air-trace the letters and then choose volunteers to write the letters on the chalkboard as you verbalize the strokes again.

22

J — Drop and hook.

j — Drop low and hook,
Dot.

V — Drop right,
Climb right.

v — Drop right,
Climb right.

Z — Glide right,
Drop left,
Glide right.

z — Glide right,
Drop left,
Glide right.

Guided Practice

Direct an alphabetizing activity on the chalkboard—Read the first column of words written on the chalkboard and then choose volunteers to write them in alphabetical order. Continue the same procedure with the remaining columns.

Guide the completion of worktext page 18—Direct a student to read the directions. Do the first alphabetizing activity with the students. Point out that in each alphabetizing activity the first word to be written is illustrated.

Optional Activity

Direct an alphabetizing activity—Write the words found below on the chalkboard. Challenge the students to write sentences by writing the words in alphabetical order on handwriting paper. Point out that the first word of each sentence is capitalized and that the second word is underlined.

1. long have All <u>giraffes</u> necks (*All giraffes have long necks.*)
2. weather honey sunny in <u>gather</u> Bees (*Bees gather honey in sunny weather.*)
3. umbrella <u>goats</u> Five jumped over the (*Five goats jumped over the umbrella.*)
4. truck our climbed into A <u>bear</u> (*A bear climbed into our truck.*)

Alphabet Time
Write each letter.

name _____

Aa	Bb	Cc
Dd	Ee	Ff	Gg	Hh
Ii	Jj	Kk	Ll	Mm
Nn	Oo	Pp	Qq	Rr
Ss	Tt	Uu	Vv	Ww
Xx	Yy	Zz		

Use with Lesson 18.

19

Materials and Preparation

Prepare:

- The following letters written in PreCursive on the chalkboard.

    (1) wol
    (2) lfy
    (3) seeb
    (4) ebA's

- Handwriting lines on the chalkboard.

——— Lesson Content ———

Introduction

Direct an alphabet sequencing activity—Choose volunteers to alphabetize each row of letters on the chalkboard. Tell the students that when the letters in each line are alphabetized they will make a word and that when the words are alphabetized they will make a sentence. *(Abe's bees fly low.)*

Skill Development

Demonstrate the formation of letters that have been difficult for your students—Verbalize the stroke of each letter as you write it on the chalkboard. Direct volunteers to write on the chalkboard the letters that begin at one o'clock.

Guided Practice

Guide the completion of worktext page 19—Emphasize consistency in slant as the students write each letter of the alphabet. Note students who need additional practice with letter formation.

Optional Activity

Direct a writing activity—Write the groups of letters found below on the chalkboard. Instruct the students to alphabetize the letters to make words and then alphabetize the words to form sentences. *(Ann's belt is lost. Arty bent his mop.)* Tell them to illustrate the sentences on the back of their paper.

etlb	*nnA's*	*si*	*olst*
enbt	*yrAt*	*sih*	*opm*

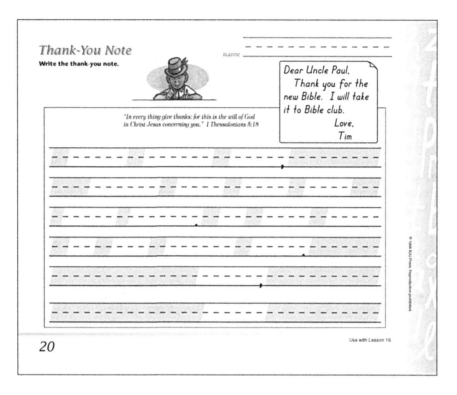

Materials and Preparation

Prepare:

- Two thank-you notes in PreCursive on chart paper, one with spacing and the other without spacing.

Note 1 (no spacing)	**Note 2** (correct spacing)
DearBill,	Dear Bill,
Thankyoufor	Thank you for
thebluetie.	the blue tie.
Love,	Love,
Joe	Joe

—————— Lesson Content ——————

Introduction

Create interest in today's lesson—Read a poem about spacing. As you read the poem, point to the thank-you note with no spacing. (The correct note should not be visible.)

> One word? No, two words, or three words or four!
> When I look closer I see there are more.
> Who in the world could this careless one be?
> Once I look closer, I know it is me.
> How could my sentence become such a mess?
> What is its meaning? I just have to guess!
> Next time I'll follow directions instead,
> Space my words neatly so they can be read.

Choose a student to attempt to read the note with the poor spacing. Display the note with the correct spacing and lead the class in reading it in unison.

Vocabulary Development

Call attention to the margin on the thank-you note—Tell the students that the blank space on the left and right sides of the paper is the margin. Emphasize that when they write on handwriting paper they should always leave a margin, a distance of 4 to 6 dashes of the midline. Stress the importance of being consistent with the length of the spaces.

> The style of paper used by your class will determine the number of dashes for a margin.

Introduce the word *indent*—Point out that the word *thank* is indented, set in from the margin. Tell the students that when writing a note or letter they should indent the first line.

Assessment

Direct the completion of worktext page 20—Discuss the illustration and verse. Choose a volunteer to read the thank-you note. Tell the students to note the space provided for them to write the note. Point out that the margin and indented areas are shaded. Instruct the class to use correct slanting and letter formation as they write their notes independently.

Optional Activity

Direct a writing activity—Ask the students to write a thank-you note on handwriting paper to someone who has been kind to them. Write these suggestions on the chalkboard:

parents/grandparents	*principal*
pastor	*neighbor*
Sunday school teacher	*friend*

Lesson 20   Correcting a Thank-You Note

Materials and Preparation

Have available:

• Handwriting paper for each student.

Prepare:

• The following thank-you note on the chalkboard.

> dear mrs. ruski,
>   thank you for taking me to the zoo
> last saturday. those monkeys were very
> funny, but i liked the tiger best
>
>   love,
>   terry

——— Lesson Content ———

Introduction

Create interest in today's lesson—Lead a discussion about courtesy. Read the following poem.

> Yes, ma'am. No, ma'am.
> That's what to say.
> Yes, sir. No, sir.
> It's just the right way.
>
> Yes, thank you! No, thank you!
> Say it with zeal!
> To kindly express
> The way that you feel.

Ask students to tell how they feel when someone thanks them for something they have done. Let students name times when they should say "thank you." Allow students to act out a few of these situations.

Skill Development

Review the rules for capitalization and punctuation—Choose a volunteer to read the thank-you note written on the chalkboard. Ask students to point out which words should be capitalized and what punctuation mark should be used at the end of each sentence.

Review the use of indentations—Point out that the first line of the note is indented. Ask students to identify the other words that are indented.

Guided Practice

Direct the writing of the thank-you note—Direct the students to write the thank-you note from the board, correcting the capitalization and punctuation mistakes. Remind them to space correctly between words.

Optional Activity

Direct a writing activity—Tell each student to write a thank-you note with no punctuation or capitalization. Let them exchange the notes with each other and then see whether they can write the new note correctly.

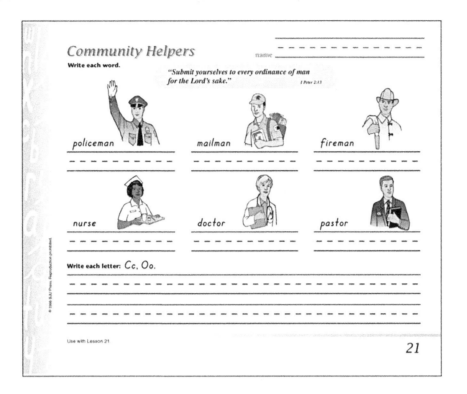

Materials and Preparation

Have available:

- One or two pictures of community helpers.

Prepare:

- Handwriting lines on the chalkboard.

———— Lesson Content ————

Introduction

Display pictures of community helpers—Discuss the jobs that these people do to make the community a good place to live. Elicit titles of other community helpers. Write each title on the chalkboard.

fireman	*doctor*
banker	*pastor*
nurse	*judge*
repairman	*market manager*
policeman	*mailman*

Skill Development

Review the formation of uppercase and lowercase *c* and *o*—As you verbalize each stroke, have a student write the letter on the chalkboard. Remind the class that these letters begin at one o'clock.

Guided Practice

Guide the completion of worktext page 21—Read and discuss I Peter 2:13. Choose volunteers to read the instructions and the names of the community helpers pictured. Instruct the students to complete only the first activity.

Work with the students as they complete the second activity. Point out that the space to be left between each group of letters is no longer shaded. Demonstrate correct spacing as you write several letters on the chalkboard.

Optional Activity

Direct a writing activity—Tell each student to write about his favorite community helper. Tell him to go on a picture hunt to see whether he can find a picture of his favorite helper in a magazine or newspaper. If magazines are not available, instruct the students to draw their own pictures.

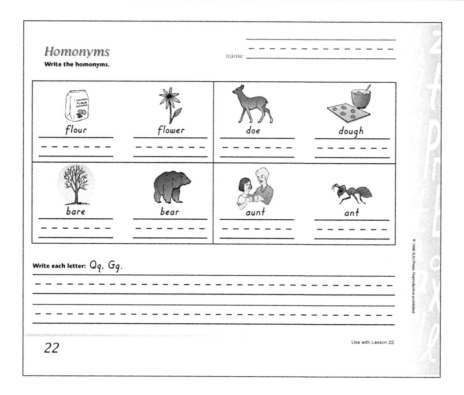

Homonyms
Write the homonyms.

name _____

flour	flower	doe	dough
bare	bear	aunt	ant

Write each letter: Qq, Gg.

22   Use with Lesson 22.

Materials and Preparation

Prepare:

- The following words in two columns on the chalkboard.

flour	*aunt*
bear	*dough*
ant	*flower*
doe	*bare*

——— Lesson Content ———

Introduction

Begin today's lesson with a matching activity—Ask the students whether they know the name given to words that are pronounced the same but spelled differently and have different meanings. *(homonyms)* Choose a volunteer to read the first word on the chalkboard and then draw a line to match it to its homonym. Then tell other students to make a sentence with each word. Continue the same procedure with the rest of the words.

Skill Development

Review the formation of uppercase and lowercase q and g—Remind the class that the letters begin at one o'clock. Direct the students to air-trace the letters as you verbalize the strokes.

Guided Practice

Direct the completion of worktext page 22—Instruct the class to read the directions silently and complete the activities independently. Remind them to space correctly as they write the letters *q* and *g*.

Optional Activity

Direct a writing activity on handwriting paper—Ask the students to see how many pairs of homonyms they can write on their papers during a given period of time. Write the following pairs on the board to help them begin.

blew	*hair*	*see*	*sail*
blue	*hare*	*sea*	*sale*

Tell each student to illustrate three of his pairs on the back of his paper. Display the students' work.

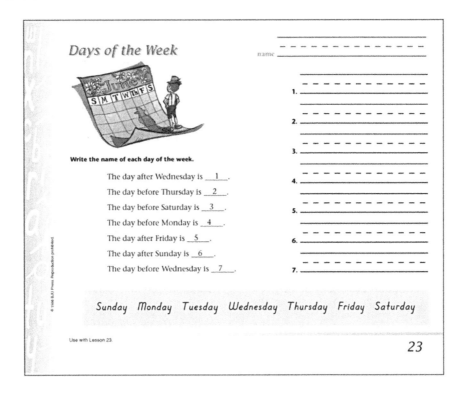

Materials and Preparation

Prepare:

- A calendar of this month.
- A word card for each day of the week.

——— Lesson Content ———

Introduction

Play a sequencing game—Scramble the word cards and display them on the chalkboard ledge. Instruct the class to read the words in unison and then direct a student to see how quickly he can put the days of the week in the correct order. Repeat the activity several times.

Skill Development

Show the students how to associate a day of the week with a date of the month—Instruct the class to look at the calendar for this month to help them answer questions such as the following:

➤ On which day of the week is October third?
➤ On which day of the week is October thirteenth?
➤ On which day of the week is October tenth?
➤ On which day of the week is October twenty-first?
➤ On which day of the week is October thirtieth?

Guided Practice

Guide the completion of worktext page 23—Choose volunteers to read the instructions and the sentences. Instruct the students to complete each sentence by writing the day of the week.

Optional Activity

Direct a writing activity—Tell the students to write Psalm 90:12 on handwriting paper. Encourage them to use correct spacing and letter formation as they write the verse from the chalkboard or chart paper.

Lesson 24   Days of the Week

Materials and Preparation

Have available:

- A calendar.
- Handwriting paper for each student.

Prepare:

- The name of each day of the week on the chalkboard, using only lowercase letters.

—— Lesson Content ——

Introduction

Create interest in today's lesson—Display a calendar for the month and ask each student who has a birthday during this month to give the date and the day of the week. Point out that on many calendars the name of each day of the week is abbreviated. Direct the students to read the names of the days of the week in unison.

Skill Development

Discuss capitalizing procedure—Tell the students that the names of the days of the week are always capitalized. Point to the words written on the chalkboard and have volunteers underline the letters that should be capitalized.

Guided Practice

Guide writing of the days of the week—Instruct the students to number their papers from 1 to 7 and then to write the days of the week correctly. Tell them to begin with Sunday.

Optional Activity

Direct writing of sentences—Direct the students to compose a sentence for each day of the week. Write some examples on the chalkboard.

Our class has art on Tuesday.

My soccer team has a game next Wednesday.

Materials and Preparation

Have available:

- Handwriting paper for each student.

Prepare:

- Handwriting lines on the chalkboard.
- On the chalkboard the following sentence, omitting spacing between words.

I can say the pledge to the Bible.

——— Lesson Content ———

Introduction

Create interest in today's lesson—Read the poem about spacing as you point to the sentence on the chalkboard.

One word? No, two words, or three words or four!
When I look closer, I see there are more.
Who in the world could this careless one be?
Once I look closer I know it is me.
How could my sentence become such a mess?
What is its meaning? I just have to guess!
Next time I'll follow directions instead,
Space my words neatly so they can be read.

Skill Development

Review correct spacing of words in a sentence—Choose a volunteer to try to read the sentence on the chalkboard. Point out that it is difficult to read a sentence when the words

are crowded together. Emphasize the importance of consistency in spacing. Tell the students that the amount of space left between any two words in a sentence should be the same. Ask another student to write the sentence correctly on the chalkboard.

Guided Practice

Guide the completion of worktext page 24—Choose volunteers to read the directions and the pledge to the Bible. Give the following instructions:

1. Write your name on the first writing line of your paper.
2. Begin the pledge on the third line.
3. Leave a margin on each line and space correctly between words.
4. Use your best PreCursive writing as you write the pledge.

Optional Activity

Direct a review activity—Write the following sentences on the chalkboard or chart paper. Do not space between the words. Explain that you have written the sentences incorrectly and then challenge the students to space the words correctly as they write the sentences on handwriting paper.

1. I carry my Bible to school every day.
2. One time I led the pledge.
3. I learned the pledge to the Bible in first grade.
4. We say the pledge every morning.

A Bible Verse
Write the verse.

name _____

In the beginning God created

the heaven and the earth.

Genesis 1:1

Write each letter: *Ss, Ee, Aa.*

Use with Lesson 26.

25

Materials and Preparation

Prepare:

• Handwriting lines on the chalkboard.

—— Lesson Content ——

Introduction

Create interest in today's lesson—Sing "The Handwriting Song."

Skill Development

Direct a review of uppercase and lowercase *s, e,* and *a*—Verbalize the direction of each stroke as several students write the letters on the chalkboard.

Guided Practice

Guide the completion of worktext page 25—Choose a volunteer to read the instructions and the verse. Tell the students to note the words that are capitalized and the punctuation mark at the end of the sentence. Remind them to space correctly as they complete the activities on this page.

Optional Activity

Direct a drawing and labeling activity—Display the Days of Creation visuals from the BJU Press Bible curriculum. Direct the students to make and label their own illustrations of the days of Creation.

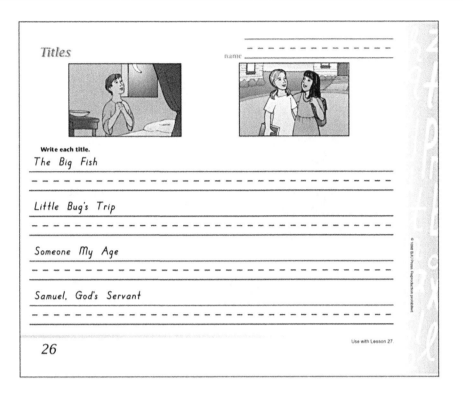

Materials and Preparation

Prepare:

- Handwriting lines on the chalkboard.

——— Lesson Content ———

Introduction

Elicit titles of favorite stories—Ask several students to name their favorite stories. As titles are dictated, write them on the chalkboard.

Skill Development

Point out the use of capitalization in titles—Direct the students' attention to the titles written on the chalkboard. Tell the students that the important words in each title begin with an uppercase letter. Choose volunteers to read the titles and point out the uppercase letters.

Review the letters that begin at one o'clock—Ask students to name the letters that have a one o'clock start. Then direct several students to demonstrate the formation of the letters on the chalkboard.

Guided Practice

Guide the completion of worktext page 26—Choose volunteers to read the instructions and story titles. After each title has been read and the students have noted the letters that should be capitalized, instruct them to write the titles correctly. Remind them to space correctly.

Optional Activity

Announce a title-writing contest—Display several bright and colorful magazine pictures. Announce that each picture needs a title. Distribute handwriting paper and have the students write a title for each picture. Collect the papers and compile a list of suggested titles for each picture. Allow the students to choose their favorite titles and then have the writer of each winning title write the title on a sentence strip. Display the pictures with their titles.

Autumn Time
Write the poem on handwriting paper.

name

Autumn Time
See what's falling all around.
Leaves of red and gold.
See what's growing on the vines.
Pumpkins bright and bold.
Summer's over. Winter's near.
Time for harvest—autumn's here!

"And he changeth the times and the seasons." Daniel 2:21

Use with Lesson 28.

27

Materials and Preparation

Have available:

- Handwriting paper for each student.
- Several seasonal poems.

> *Favorite Poems Old and New* by Helen Ferris is available from BJU Press.

Prepare:

- Handwriting lines on the chalkboard.

———— Lesson Content ————

Introduction

Create interest in today's lesson—Read several poems that tell about a season. Choose a student to read the first phrase of Daniel 2:21. Discuss the concept that God is in control of the change of seasons.

Skill Development

Guide a review of letters that have a serif—Tell students to demonstrate the serif by standing on their tiptoes. Choose a volunteer to write on the chalkboard the PreCursive letters that end in a serif.

Guided Practice

Guide the completion of worktext page 27—Read the poem to the class. Then tell the class to read it in unison. Point out the use of uppercase letters and punctuation marks. Before the students begin writing the poem on handwriting paper, remind them to leave a margin on the left and right sides of their papers and to space correctly between the words.

Optional Activity

Direct a writing and art activity—Remind the students of the colors named in the poem "Autumn Time." Instruct them to compose sentences about their favorite fall color and then to use all the colors to draw a fall scene. Collect the papers and make a book for the students to enjoy during their free time.

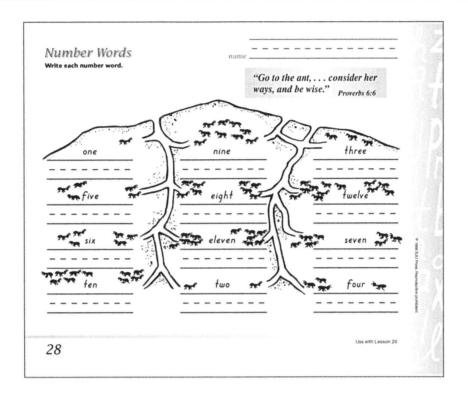

Materials and Preparation

Prepare:

- Handwriting lines on the chalkboard.
- The number words *one* to *twelve* on the chalkboard.

——— Lesson Content ———

Introduction

Lead a pantomiming activity—Read the first two stanzas of the poem "Writing Time" and have the students pantomime the words.

> Guess what! Writing time is here!
> Make your desk all clean and clear.
> Get your paper, pencil too;
> Listen now for what to do.
>
> Sit up tall and plant your feet.
> Make quite sure your paper's neat.
> Take your pencil; hold it right,
> Not too loose and not too tight.

Skill Development

Guide a review of lowercase letters that have a descender—Tell several students to name lowercase letters that have a descender and to write them on the chalkboard. Point out the letters that have identical descenders. Provide additional practice of these letters on the chalkboard for students who do not write them correctly.

Review number words—Direct a student to read the first number word written on the chalkboard. Instruct another student to write the numeral that represents the number word. Continue the same procedure with the rest of the words.

Guided Practice

Guide the completion of worktext page 28—Read Proverbs 6:6 in unison and discuss the meaning of the verse. Ask how many students have seen a colony of ants at work. Tell the students that ants are hard workers and that they never delay doing work. Encourage the students to be like the ants as they complete their daily assignments. Instruct them to do their neatest work as they write the number words on their worktext page.

Optional Activity

Direct writing of a verse—Distribute handwriting paper and direct the students to write Proverbs 6:6.

35

Capitalization   name _____

Write each sentence correctly.

ants are diligent workers.

they aid the farmer by loosening the soil.

they prepare for the winter by gathering food in summer.

There are over 20,000 species of ants.
An ant can carry a load many times heavier than itself.

Write each letter: *Dd.*

Use with Lesson 30.

29

Materials and Preparation

Prepare:

- Handwriting lines on the chalkboard.
- The following sentences on the chalkboard without capitalizing the first word in each sentence.

  Ants live in colonies.
  Ants do not have bones.
  The anteater is an enemy of the ants.

——— Lesson Content ———

Introduction

Create interest in today's lesson—Ask whether any of the students have watched ants at work. Ask whether the ants remind the students of a bustling crowd or a marching army. Let them share some of their ideas. Elicit the following information:

  An ant is a small insect.
  An ant is dark brown, black, or red.
  An ant lives in a colony.
  An ant's body is divided into three parts.
  An ant has no bones.

Skill Development

Discuss capitalizing the first word in a sentence—Ask students to name the uses of capital letters. Write these rules on the chalkboard as students dictate. Include the following: beginning of names, beginning of sentences, important words in titles, first word in every line of poetry, and the names of God.

Guided Practice

Guide the completion of worktext page 29—Choose a volunteer to read the interesting facts about ants. Elicit from the students which words need to be capitalized and which two sentences require more than one writing line because of their length. Remind them that the punctuation mark indicates the end of a sentence. Encourage the students to use their neatest PreCursive writing as they complete the activity.

Optional Activity

Direct writing of facts about insects—Tell the students to choose an insect from the list on the chalkboard. (Include the following: fly, lightning bug, mosquito, and caterpillar.) Instruct the students to write three facts about the one they chose. Give them an example:

  Mosquito
  1. Mosquitoes live near water.
  2. They have six legs.
  3. Mosquitoes live from seventeen to thirty days.

Lesson 31   A Review

Materials and Preparation

Prepare:

- Handwriting lines on the chalkboard.
- The following sentence on the chalkboard.

  Ants are diligent workers.

—— Lesson Content ——

Introduction

Create interest in today's lesson—Sing "The Handwriting Song."

Skill Development

Review letters that end with a serif—Write the lowercase *a* on the chalkboard. Remind the students that the letter *a* is made with one stroke and that the ending of the stroke bends to the line with a slight curve called a serif. Trace the serif with colored chalk. Have a student read the sentence written on the chalkboard and underline the letters that end with a serif.

Guided Practice

Guide writing of letters with a serif—Distribute handwriting paper and instruct the students to write the PreCursive letters that end with a serif. Then challenge the students to see how many words they can write with these letters.

Optional Activity

Direct writing of one-stroke letters—Direct the students to write the letters that are made with one stroke. Tell them to underline the letters that begin at one o'clock and to draw a line above the letters that end with a serif.

Unusual Clocks

Write the name of each clock.

name _____

Skeleton Clock

Lighthouse Clock

Write each letter: *Ii, Ll, Tt.*

30

Use with Lesson 32.

Materials and Preparation

Prepare:

- Handwriting lines on the chalkboard.

——— Lesson Content ———

Introduction

Create interest in today's lesson—Lead a discussion about unusual clocks. Ask the students whether they have an unusual clock at home or whether they have a friend or neighbor who owns an unusual clock. Tell the students that they will see some very unusual clocks in today's lesson.

Skill Development

Review the formation of uppercase and lowercase *i*, *l*, and *t*—Verbalize the direction of the strokes as you write each letter on the chalkboard. Let several students write the letters on the chalkboard.

Guided Practice

Guide the completion of worktext page 30—Point out the unusual clocks shown on page 30. Share the following information with the class:

> The lighthouse clock was made in the 1800s. The clock dial is in the body of the lighthouse. On the top is a rotating lamp.

> The most typical feature of the French skeleton clock is a large main wheel. The clock stands on a wooden base. There is a clock-making firm in England that still manufactures skeleton clocks.

Ask a student to read the directions for both exercises and let the class work independently on the activities.

Optional Activity

Direct composing of a description—Tell the students to write a short description of the clock on page 30 that they think is the most unusual.

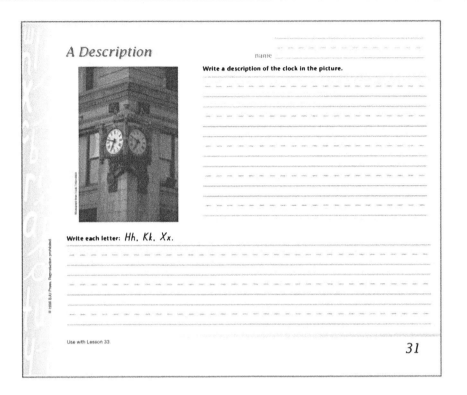

Materials and Preparation

Have available:

- The Timothy Time puppet.

Prepare:

- Handwriting lines on the chalkboard.
- A short description of a clock on the chalkboard, similar to the following.

  We have a big, round, daisy clock at our house. The yellow and white clock hangs on the kitchen wall. It tells us when it is time to eat.

———— Lesson Content ————

Introduction

Create interest in today's lesson—Use Timothy Time to read the following rhyme:

> Timothy Time has a clock truly fine;
> It ticks and it tocks and it tells him to dine,
> For it hangs in the kitchen, it hangs on the wall,
> With its minute hand large and its hour hand small.

Skill Development

Review the formation of uppercase and lowercase *h, k,* and *x*—Verbalize the direction of the strokes as you write each letter on the chalkboard. Choose volunteers to write the letters on the chalkboard.

Guided Practice

Motivate the children to write—Read the clock description that you have written on the chalkboard. Allow several children to describe a clock that they have at home.

Guide the completion of worktext page 31—Direct the students' attention to the picture of a clock. Allow volunteers to give a verbal description of the clock. Then instruct a student to read the directions for the activities on the worktext page. Circulate among the students as they write the description. When the students have completed the activity, allow them to read their descriptions to the class.

Optional Activity

Direct an illustrating and composing activity—Instruct the students to illustrate a clock that they have at home. Tell them to write the numerals *1* through *12* on the face of their clock. Then direct them to write a description of their clock on handwriting paper.

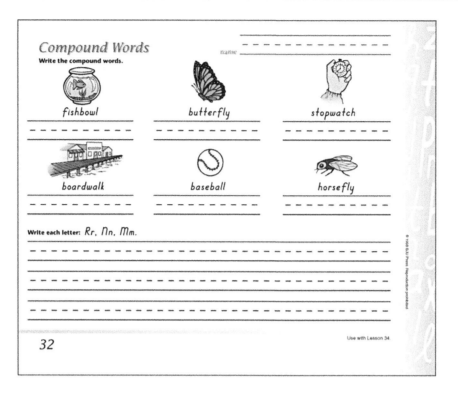

Materials and Preparation

Prepare:

• The following words in PreCursive on the chalkboard.

wind	case
book	mill
police	coat
rain	man

——— Lesson Content ———

Introduction

Create interest in today's lesson—Use the tune "Did You Ever See a Lassie?" to introduce compound words. Tell the students that a compound word is two words put together to make one new word. Instruct them to listen for the compound word that you will substitute for the word *lassie.* Sing: "Did you ever see a horsefly, a horsefly, a horsefly? Did you ever see a horsefly? Now you tell us one." Point out the double meaning behind the compound word—a horse cannot fly, but a horsefly is a type of insect with wings. Then allow volunteers to sing the song using the following compound words: *shoestring, baseball, bedspread, butterfly, and toothbrush.*

Skill Development

Discuss the definition of a compound word—Tell the students that many of the words they use are compound words. Instruct them to read the words written on the chalkboard and then allow volunteers to form compound words by drawing lines to connect the words. After the lines have been drawn, tell the students to respond in unison to the following questions:

Where are books kept? *(bookcase)*
What do you wear on a rainy day? *(raincoat)*
What do you call a man who is employed to enforce the law? *(policeman)*
What do we call a mill used to pump water? *(windmill)*

Guided Practice

Guide the completion of worktext page 32—Ask for a volunteer to read the directions for both exercises. As the students write the compound words, move around the room and check to make sure that they are practicing correct writing posture, paper position, and pencil hold. Instruct the students to complete the work at the bottom of the page independently.

Optional Activity

Direct a writing activity—Tell the students to make a list of all the compound words they can think of. Help them begin the list with the words *firefly* and *lighthouse.*

Lesson 35   Compound Words

Materials and Preparation

Have available:

- Handwriting paper for each student.

Prepare:

- Handwriting lines on the chalkboard.
- The following list of words in PreCursive on the chalkboard.

bulldogs	*circus*	*hornet*
buffalo	*classroom*	*gingerbread*
inchworm	*donkey*	*lumberjack*
careful	*footstep*	*pigpen*

Lesson Content

Introduction

Lead an activity using compound words—Write the word *inside* on the chalkboard, and then choose a volunteer to use the word in a sentence. If the word is used correctly, allow that student to write a compound word on the chalkboard; then call on another student to use it in a sentence. Continue the same procedure until several compound words have been written on the chalkboard.

Skill Development

Direct a discrimination activity—Point out the words written on the chalkboard. Allow volunteers to tell the class which words are compound words. For those that are compound words, let students show where they can be divided to make two words.

Guided Practice

Direct a defining activity—Tell the students to write the compound words listed on the chalkboard. As time allows, let them write definitions for these words.

Optional Activity

Direct the composing of a short story—Allow the students to use the other side of their paper to write a short story using a compound word of their choice. Create interest in writing by reading the following story to the class:

> One day as Kelly Kangaroo began to prepare lunch, she tripped on the rug. The butter in her hand flew out the window and landed on a flower. "Did you see my butterfly?" Kelly asked.

Let the students pick out the compound word in the story. Direct them in choosing one of their own to fit into the story.

Materials and Preparation

Prepare:

- The initials of several students in PreCursive on the chalkboard.

———— Lesson Content ————

Introduction

Sing "The Handwriting Song."

Skill Development

Review uppercase and lowercase *d, k, n,* and *m*—Tell the students to write the letters on the chalkboard as you verbalize each stroke.

Direct a game to reinforce the use of initials—Point out the initials you have written on the chalkboard. Choose a volunteer to guess the name of the person represented by the first set of initials. Continue until all are guessed. Point out that initials are the first letter of the students' first and last names and that the letters are always capitalized and followed by a period. If time permits, play a game using the students' initials. Tell the class to listen carefully as a student gives his initials and then the initials of one of his classmates. The classmate is to stand quickly, give his initials, and then give the initials of another classmate. If a classmate fails to respond quickly, the student who called his initials calls on someone else. The student should say, "My initials are ____. Your initials are ____."

Guided Practice

Guide the completion of worktext page 33—Read the directions to the class. Circulate among the students to check their work.

Optional Activity

Direct a writing activity—Instruct the students to write the initials of five classmates on handwriting paper. Remind them to capitalize each letter and to put a period after each initial.

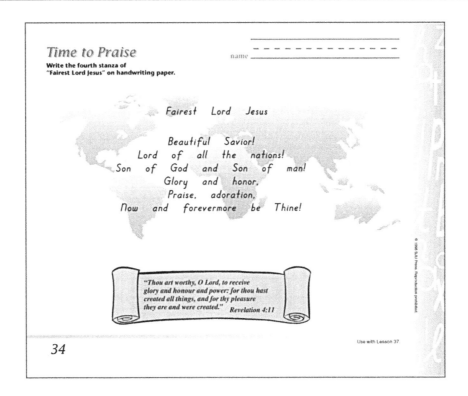

Materials and Preparation

Have available:

- Handwriting paper for each student.

Prepare:

- The hymn title "Fairest Lord Jesus" written three times on the chalkboard. Show one spaced incorrectly, one written with poor letter formation, and one written and spaced correctly.

——— Lesson Content ———

Introduction

Generate interest by humming the first few lines of "Fairest Lord Jesus"—Allow the students to guess the name of the song. Give the students the background of the song, explaining that many believe that knights once sang this song as they marched hundreds of miles to Jerusalem. Lead the class in singing "Fairest Lord Jesus."

Skill Development

Demonstrate correct spacing for a title—Direct attention to the titles on the chalkboard. Ask the students what is wrong with the first title. Choose a student to write it correctly on the chalkboard. Continue with the second one, then compare both with the correctly written third title.

Assessment

Direct the completion of worktext page 34—Ask a student to read Revelation 4:11 to the class. Discuss the verse with the class. Tell the class to read the last stanza of the song in unison, then write it on handwriting paper. Encourage the students to evaluate their handwriting. Tell them to mark places where words are too close or too far apart. Collect the papers and assess them according to slant, spacing, and letter formation.

Optional Activity

Direct the writing of a verse—Instruct the students to write Revelation 4:11 from the worktext page.

A Bible Verse

name _____

Blessed   is   the   nation
whose   God   is   the   Lord.
            Psalm   33:12

Write the verse.

Write each letter: *Uu, Ww, Yy.*

Use with Lesson 38

35

Materials and Preparation

Have available:

- A map of the United States or a globe.

Prepare:

- Handwriting lines on the chalkboard.
- The first half of Psalm 33:12 in cursive on the chalkboard.

—— Lesson Content ——

Introduction

Create interest in today's lesson—Display a map or globe for the class. Help the students locate their country on it. Point out that their country, the United States of America, is located on the large continent of North America. Help the students find the state they live in and the approximate location of the city or town they live in. If time permits, allow several volunteers to show where grandparents or other relatives live.

Skill Development

Guide the reading of a verse written in cursive letters— Direct the class to the first half of Psalm 33:12 on the chalkboard. Read the verse and then have the class read it in unison. Point out that the PreCursive letters are visible in most of the cursive letters. Call on students to name each letter as you point to it. Circle the cursive letters that do not have the PreCursive letter visible in them. Tell the class that soon they will learn to write the letters in cursive. Encourage them to use their best PreCursive until the cursive letters are introduced.

Guided Practice

Guide the completion of worktext page 35—Point out to the students the outline of their nation. Instruct the class to write the verse and the letters *u, w,* and *y* neatly in PreCursive. If you notice students having difficulty with any letters, provide additional practice for them on handwriting paper.

Optional Activity

Guide an illustrating and labeling activity—Provide students with state travel information brochures. Help them find the symbols that represent their state—the flower, bird, tree, motto, and so on. Let them illustrate and label these symbols.

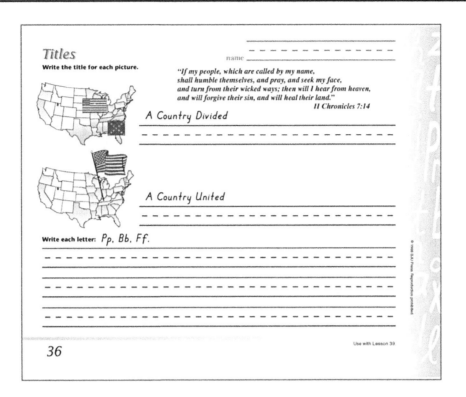

Materials and Preparation

Have available:

- A map of the United States.

Prepare:

- The following titles in cursive on the chalkboard.

  A Country Divided   *A Country United*

——— Lesson Content ———

Introduction

Generate interest with a brief history lesson—Read the titles written in cursive on the chalkboard. Tell the students that when you tap on the chalkboard and point to a title, they are to read it in unison. Practice reading the titles one time before reading the following information.

After the United States became a nation, the country grew larger and larger until there were thirty-three states. Many people worked in the factories in the North. Other people worked on the farms in the South. Each part began to have problems, and the people of the South decided to become a separate nation. (Tap the chalkboard and point to the title "A Country Divided." Tell the children to read the title in unison.)

When Abraham Lincoln was president, the arguing between the North and South finally became a war. The war lasted four years. Many people died in the war, which ended in 1865. Then this nation was reunited into one strong country. (Tap on the board and point to the title "A Country United." Tell the children to read the title in unison.)

Skill Development

Direct the students in noting the similarities and differences between PreCursive and cursive letters—Select students to draw a line under the letters in the two titles that are similar to the PreCursive letters.

Review rules for capitalization—Remind the students that the first word and all important words in a title are capitalized.

Guided Practice

Guide the completion of worktext page 36—Ask for a volunteer to read the directions for the writing activities. Read II Chronicles 7:14 in unison. Remind the students to use correct spacing and letter formation as they write. Walk around the room, checking for problems, particularly with *p, b,* and *f.*

Optional Activity

Direct a writing and illustrating activity—Tell the students to write the following titles on handwriting paper. Instruct them to make a book jacket by cutting out the titles, gluing them to construction paper, and then illustrating them.

The Life of Abraham Lincoln
The War Between the States
Our Strong America

American Patriots   name _____

Patriotism is showing love to one's country.

A patriot is one who loves and serves his country.

Write the sentence.

Mount   Rushmore   shows   men   who   were American   patriots.

Write each letter: Vv, Zz.

Use with Lesson 40

37

Materials and Preparation

Have available:

- A dictionary.

Prepare:

- The word *patriot* in PreCursive on the chalkboard.
- Several students' names in cursive on the chalkboard.

———— Lesson Content ————

Introduction

Generate interest by discussing the word *patriot*—Ask the students what they think the word means. Guide a student in looking up the word in the dictionary. Show the class that a patriot is a person who loves, supports, and defends his country. Ask for the patriots in the class to raise their hands.

Skill Development

Guide the reading of names written in cursive letters—Instruct the class to read the names on the chalkboard. Let each child whose name is written on the chalkboard circle all the cursive letters in his name that differ from the Pre-Cursive model. Review the concept that the first letter in a person's name is always capitalized.

Guided Practice

Guide the completion of worktext page 37—Assist the students with the identification of each American patriot. Tell the class that George Washington was our first president and that Abraham Lincoln was the president who helped unite the states after they divided. Also tell them that Theodore Roosevelt was the president who saved much of our land for parks and that because of his love of nature the teddy bear was named for him. Thomas Jefferson was our third president and helped write the Declaration of Independence. Explain that all these American presidents loved their country. Ask a volunteer to read the directions for completing the activities on this page. Have the class read the sentence in unison. Remind the students that they must demonstrate correct letter formation and spacing before they begin cursive writing.

Optional Activity

Direct a writing activity—Write the names of both the president of the United States and the governor of your state on the chalkboard. Tell the students to write these names on handwriting paper.

Lesson 41   America's Parks

Materials and Preparation

Have available:

* Handwriting paper for each student.

Prepare:

* Handwriting lines on the chalkboard.

——— Lesson Content ———

Introduction

Lead a discussion about national forests and parks—Ask whether anyone has ever climbed a tree. Tell the class that many trees are protected in national forests. The trees are kept safe for us to enjoy. Name some of the national forests in your area. Ask whether any students have camped in a national forest. Tell the class that some of these forests are destroyed each year because of carelessness; people often start fires that burn trees and animal homes. Relate the story of Smokey the Bear, telling that firefighters rescued him from a forest fire, that doctors treated his burns, and that he became a symbol for preventing forest fires as Americans heard his story. Tell the students that Smokey the Bear's motto is "Only you can prevent forest fires."

Skill Development

Review the letters that your class needs additional practice writing—Verbalize the stroke direction as you write each letter on the chalkboard.

Guided Practice

Direct writing on handwriting paper—Tell the students to list ways they can prevent forest fires. Write these suggestions on the chalkboard as students dictate. Instruct the class to write these rules for fire prevention on handwriting paper.

Optional Activity

Direct writing of mottoes—Tell the students to write Smokey the Bear's motto: "Only you can prevent forest fires." Encourage them to write several additional mottoes that apply to fire prevention at your school (e.g., "Don't play with matches!").

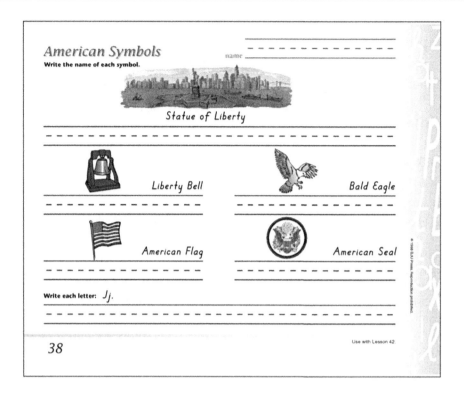

Materials and Preparation

Have available:

- An American flag.

Prepare:

- Handwriting lines on the chalkboard.
- The following scrambled words in PreCursive on the chalkboard.

ellb	*gaele*	*agfl*	*esal*
(bell)	(eagle)	(flag)	(seal)

——— Lesson Content ———

Introduction

Generate interest by explaining what a symbol is—Tell the class that a symbol is a sign or object that stands for something. Point to the American flag, explaining that it is one of this nation's most important symbols. Discuss the meaning of the different parts of the flag. Red stands for courage, white for purity, and blue for justice. The stripes stand for the thirteen original states and the stars for each state in the Union. Tell the students that this country has several other important symbols, which they will see in this lesson.

Skill Development

Review the letters that end with a serif—Direct the students to point out on the handwriting charts the letters that

have a serif. Remind them that a serif is a curve similar to the one formed by their toes when standing tiptoe.

Direct the students to write letters that end with a serif—Point out the scrambled words on the chalkboard. Tell the class that each word names one of the American symbols. Unscramble the first word and then challenge three students to see how quickly they can unscramble the words and write them neatly on the chalkboard. Let the class check their spelling and evaluate their handwriting. Allow other students to underline the letters that have a serif.

Guided Practice

Guide the completion of worktext page 38—Direct a student to read the directions. Remind the students to use correct spacing between the words and the letters at the bottom of the page as they write.

Optional Activity

Direct a writing activity—Tell the students to unscramble and write the following words on handwriting paper:

dre	(red)
ulbe	(blue)
thiwe	(white)
glaf	(flag)

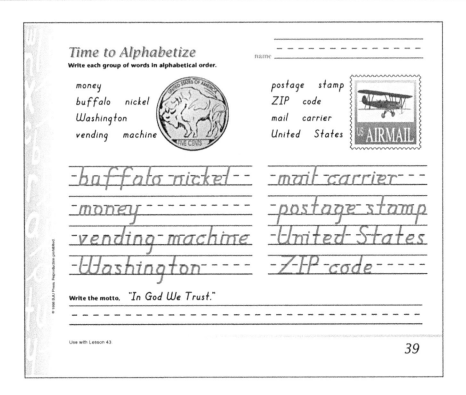

Materials and Preparation

Prepare:

- The following words in cursive on the chalkboard.

  Statue of Liberty
  Liberty Bell
  American seal
  Bald eagle
  American flag

——— Lesson Content ———

Introduction

Generate interest by singing "The Handwriting Song"—
Tell the girls to sing the first stanza as the boys pantomime
the words. Then tell the boys to sing the second stanza while
the girls pantomime the words.

Skill Development

Review the lowercase letters having a descender—Elicit
the names of lowercase letters having a descender. Allow
students to write them on the chalkboard.

Direct an alphabetizing activity—Instruct a student to
read the names of the symbols that are written on the
chalkboard. Point out that they will have to refer to the
second word when alphabetizing the names of the two
symbols that begin with *American*. Tell a student to choose
which word comes first in alphabetical order and then write
the numeral *1* beside it. Continue the same procedure until
all words are alphabetized.

Guided Practice

Guide the completion of worktext page 39—Choose a
volunteer to read the directions. Instruct the students to
complete the page as you walk around the room helping
those with individual problems.

Optional Activity

Direct an alphabetizing activity—Instruct the students to
alphabetize the following words on handwriting paper:

patriot	*red*
loyal	*white*
United States	*blue*

Materials and Preparation

Have available:

- Handwriting paper for each child.

——— Lesson Content ———

Introduction

Lead the class in singing—Sing "My Country, 'Tis of Thee" with the students; then tell the class that this song was written in the 1800s. Explain that the first time it was sung was at a children's Fourth-of-July picnic; since then children have always enjoyed singing it.

Skill Development

Guide reading of cursive writing—Remind the students of the symbols pictured on page 38 of the worktext. Use cursive as you write the name of each symbol on the chalkboard. Then allow several students to read the words in cursive.

Assessment

Direct the completion of worktext page 40—Tell the students that the handwriting exercise for today is important because it is the last PreCursive lesson. Tell the students to write the first verse of "My Country, 'Tis of Thee" on handwriting paper. Remind the class that the first letter of every line is capitalized. Tell them to be careful to put in the correct punctuation marks also. Assess the papers according to slant, spacing, neatness, and letter formation. Note progress that students have made by comparing this assessment to the Pretest.

Optional Activity

Direct a writing activity—Instruct the students to write the fourth verse of "My Country, 'Tis of Thee" on handwriting paper.

> Our fathers' God to Thee,
> Author of liberty,
> To Thee we sing:
> Long may our land be bright
> With freedom's holy light;
> Protect us by Thy might,
> Great God, our King!

Lesson 45   A Posttest

Materials and Preparation

Have available:

- The students' pretests from Lesson 3.
- Handwriting paper for each student.

———— Lesson Content ————

Introduction

Discuss the students' progress in handwriting—Compliment them for their good work. List areas of improvement on the chalkboard. Include the following: letter formation, spacing, alignment, slant, and neatness.

Posttest

Direct a posttest—Distribute handwriting paper and direct the students to write the uppercase and lowercase letters of the alphabet.

Guide the students in contrasting present writing with past writing—Distribute students' pretests. Before collecting the papers, instruct each student to look at his pretest and encourage each student to note his own improvement in handwriting.

Optional Activity

Direct a letter-writing activity—Direct the students as they write a letter to their parents. You may write the following letter on the board for the students to use as a model.

[date]

Dear Mother and Dad,

On [day] our class will begin cursive writing. It will be easy to learn. [Teacher's name] will teach me how to connect the PreCursive letters that I have learned. Then I'll be able to write like you. I'm so excited!

Love,
[Student's name]

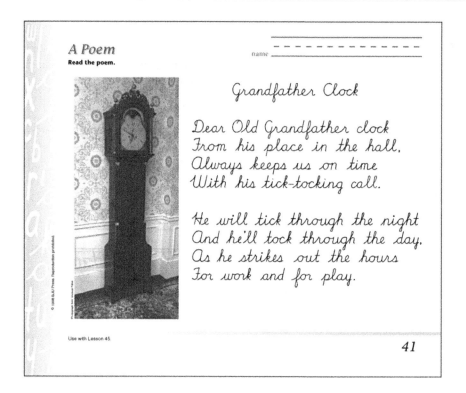

Materials and Preparation

Have available:

- Timothy Time puppet with his new clothes (Appendix, p. A17).

Prepare:

- The cursive handwriting charts by placing them underneath the PreCursive charts.

——— Lesson Content ———

Introduction

Sing "The Handwriting Song."

Introduce the cursive handwriting charts—Read the following poem as Timothy Time, dressed in his new hat and jacket, points to the cursive letters displayed in front of the classroom.

> Now the dress-up day is here.
> Cursive letters will appear.
> With one stroke that joins and flows,
> Writing wears its grown-up clothes.

Skill Development

Guide the reading of cursive letters—Point out that most PreCursive letters are visible in the cursive letters. Lead the students as they read the cursive letters in unison.

Introduce the cursive stroke—Direct the students' attention to the lowercase cursive letter *c*. Point out that the PreCursive letter is visible in the cursive letter. Tell the students that the stroke that "dresses up the PreCursive letter" is called the cursive stroke and that it will serve as the connecting stroke when letters are joined in a word. Instruct students to name other lowercase letters that have the cursive stroke.

Demonstrate the formation of a letter with the cursive stroke—Write a large lowercase cursive letter *c* on the chalkboard. Trace the cursive stroke with colored chalk as you point out that the cursive stroke for this letter begins at the baseline and then swings up and around to one o'clock. Tell the students to stand and air-trace the cursive stroke.

Write another lowercase cursive letter *c* on the chalkboard and tell the students to note that the cursive stroke and the stroke of the PreCursive letter are combined and that the cursive letter is formed with one continuing stroke.

Guided Practice

Guide air-tracing of a letter with the cursive stroke—Direct the students to stand and air-trace the lowercase cursive letter *c* as you verbalize the stroke.

> Swing up and around to one,
> Retrace and swing around to five.

Guide the completion of worktext page 41—Ask if anyone has a grandfather clock at home. Discuss the clock's characteristics (height, sound, winding). Choose a volunteer to read the title of the poem. Point out the cursive letters in the title that differ from the PreCursive model. As you read the poem, tell the students to underline letters that they do not recognize. Then allow several students to read the poem as you circulate around the classroom and identify letters for them. Conclude the lesson by having the class read the poem in unison.

Optional Activity

Direct composing of a story—Write the following story titles in PreCursive on the chalkboard. Instruct the students to choose a title and write a story about it. Tell them to use their best PreCursive writing.

The Boy Who Found the Clock
The Grandfather Clock That Would Not Chime
My Grandfather's Clock
The Broken Clock Face
The Clock with the Missing Hands

Do not permit students to write words in cursive until they have been taught the correct way to write each letter.

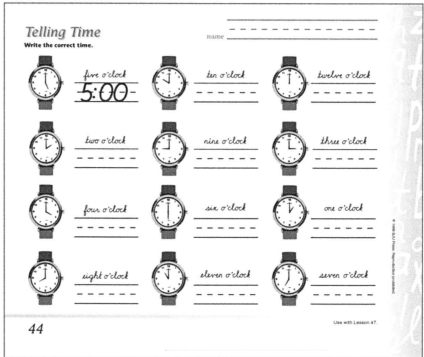

Materials and Preparation

Prepare:

• The poem "Writing Time" in cursive on chart paper.

> The poem will be used in several lessons.

——— Lesson Content ———

Introduction

Create interest in today's lesson—Ask for a volunteer to read the poem "Writing Time."

Guess what! Writing time is here!
Make your desk all clean and clear.
Get your paper, pencil too;
Listen now for what to do.

Sit up tall and plant your feet.
Make quite sure your paper's neat.
Take your pencil; hold it right,
Not too loose and not too tight.

Don't be jerky; don't be slow.
Let your pencil glide and flow.
Letters lean but do not fall;
Not too big, but not too small.

Throughout the lesson acknowledge publicly those who follow the advice in the poem.

Pretest

Guide the completion of the pretest on worktext page 43—Instruct the students to read the letters on page 42 in unison. Point out that the cursive stroke for each lowercase letter begins at the baseline. Show how the stroke swings up and flows into the PreCursive letter *b*. Choose a student to read the directions on page 43. Tell the class that they are going to try to write the letters of the alphabet in cursive handwriting. Tell them to use the models on page 42 as a guide. Encourage the students to attempt each letter but not to spend a long time on each one. Remind the students that the pretest will not be graded or sent home, but will be saved for them to see their progress as they learn the correct way to write each letter.

Guide the completion of the numeral pretest on worktext page 44—Allow a volunteer to read the directions. Direct the students to read the words under the first clock and finger-trace the numerals. Instruct the class to complete the page. Tell the students to refer to the inside front cover for correct formation of the numerals.

Collect the papers. Record pertinent observations, using the following checklist:

Which letters are the most difficult for students to write and may require more than one lesson to teach?

Which students need additional activities at school and at home to strengthen fine muscle coordination?

Which students have difficulty with alignment, spacing, and slant?

Which students do not write the lowercase letters with one continuous stroke?

Which students confuse the direction of the stroke?

Optional Activity

Direct an art activity—Tell the students to draw a clock mural on a large piece of art paper. Tell them to draw pictures depicting what they do at various hours of the day.

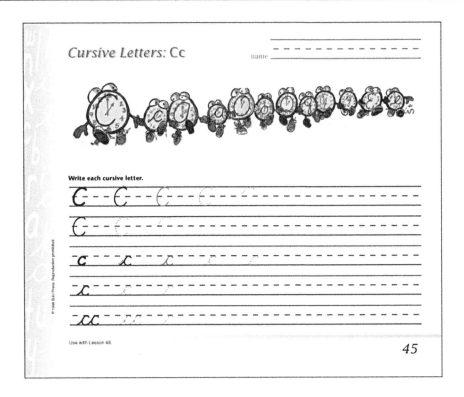

Materials and Preparation

Prepare:

- Handwriting lines on the chalkboard.
- The following words in PreCursive on the chalkboard:

  cactus   circus   Canada   Christian

- A picture on the chalkboard similar to the following.

——— Lesson Content ———

Introduction

Create interest in connecting letters in cursive—Point out the picture on the chalkboard. Ask the students what letter is making the waves. *(c)* Explain that in cursive writing letters are connected to form a continuous line.

Skill Development

Demonstrate the formation of uppercase and lowercase cursive *c*—Point to the uppercase cursive *c* on the handwriting charts. Ask the children if that *c* is different from or the same as the PreCursive *c*. Point out that it is the same. Ask

at what clock position *c* starts *(one o'clock)*. Point out the lowercase cursive *c* on the handwriting charts. Ask if it is different from or the same as the PreCursive form, having them point out the cursive stroke in front. Verbalize the direction of the strokes as you write each letter on the chalkboard.

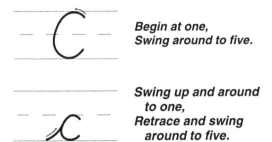

Begin at one,
Swing around to five.

Swing up and around
to one,
Retrace and swing
around to five.

Demonstrate the writing of lowercase *c* in pairs—Point out that the pencil is not lifted between the letters. Tell the class to air-trace the letter *c* in pairs and then have several students practice writing pairs of the letter *c* on the chalkboard.

Demonstrate connecting of the letters in a word—Choose a student to read the words on the chalkboard. Then write the words in cursive writing and point out that both the uppercase and lowercase *c* connect to the lowercase letters that follow them.

Guided Practice

Guide the completion of worktext page 45—Call attention to the clock family of one o'clock letters. Ask the students whether they see any similarity between the PreCursive and cursive models. Remind them to note the arrow that indicates the direction of the stroke before they trace the gray and dotted models. Point out that on the bottom line they are to write the letter *c* in pairs. Remind the students that they must let their pencils flow by not picking them up between letters.

Circulate among the students as they complete the worktext page and note those who need additional practice with writing letters in pairs.

Optional Activity

Direct a tracking activity—Prepare a copy for each student of the picture you drew on the chalkboard. Encourage the students to finger-trace the *c*s.

Lesson 49   Cursive Letters: *Aa*   Worktext page 46

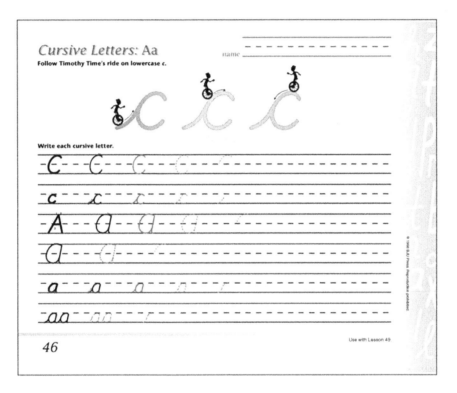

Materials and Preparation

Prepare:
- Handwriting lines on the chalkboard.
- The following words in PreCursive on the chalkboard.

     America   *star*   *age*

———— Lesson Content ————

Introduction

Generate interest by composing tongue twisters—Encourage the class to think of words beginning with the letter *c*. Combine these to make tongue twisters (e.g., *Clara's clothespins clip clean clothes*). Write several of the tongue twisters on the chalkboard.

Skill Development

Demonstrate the formation of uppercase and lowercase *a*—Review the formation of the letter *c*. Point out that the beginning of the stroke for *a* is the same as for *c*. Verbalize the direction of the strokes as you write each letter on the chalkboard.

Begin at one,
Swing around to lock,
Retrace and curve.

Swing up and around
*   to one,*
Retrace and swing
*   around to lock,*
Retrace and curve.

57

Demonstrate the writing of lowercase *a* in pairs—Point out that the pencil is not lifted between the letters. Tell the class to air-trace the letter *a* in pairs and then allow several students to practice writing pairs of letter *a* on the chalkboard.

Demonstrate the connecting of the letters in words—Choose students to read the words on the chalkboard. Then write the words in cursive writing and point out that both the uppercase and lowercase *a* connect to the lowercase letters that follow them.

Guided Practice

Guide the completion of worktext page 46—Choose a volunteer to read the directions at the top of the page. Ask whether anyone knows what kind of vehicle Timothy Time is riding. *(unicycle)* Tell the students to finger-trace Timothy Time's ride. Point out the similarities and differences of the PreCursive and cursive *c* and *a*. Point out that the pairs of *a*s need special care with spacing and connecting. Observe individual students closely, checking their letter formation as they write.

Optional Activity

Reinforce letter formation—Fill the lid of a shoebox or a tray with sand. Direct the children to practice the formation of cursive *c* and *a* by finger-tracing in the sand.

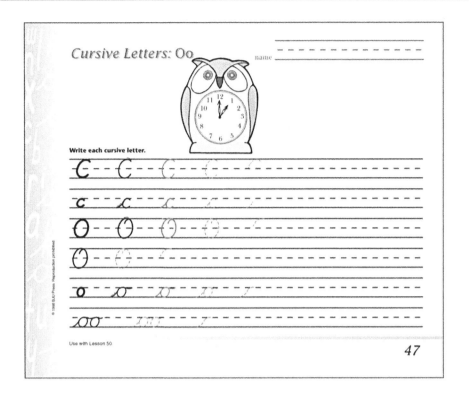

Materials and Preparation

Prepare:

- Handwriting lines on the chalkboard.
- The following words in PreCursive on the chalkboard.

    book   *owl*   *Ollie*

——— Lesson Content ———

Introduction

Use a riddle to create interest—Read the following riddle to the class:

> Today we'll write a brand new vowel,
> With the help of wise old owl.
> Within his name you'll find a clue.
> It's not an *a, e, i,* or *u.*

Give the students an opportunity to guess the new letter. Tell them the letter is used at the beginning of *old* and *owl.*

Skill Development

Demonstrate the formation of cursive *o*—Review the formation of cursive *c.* Compare cursive *o* to *c.* Verbalize the direction of the strokes as you write the letter *o* on the chalkboard. Then allow several students to write the letters on the chalkboard.

Begin at one,
Swing around to
lock and curl.

Swing up around
to one,
Retrace and swing
around to lock,
Sweep out.

Demonstrate the writing of lowercase *o* in pairs—Point out that the pencil is not lifted between the letters. Tell the class to air-trace the letter *o* in pairs and then allow several students to practice writing pairs of the letter *o* on the chalkboard.

Demonstrate the connecting of the letters in words—Choose a student to read the words on the chalkboard. Then write the words in cursive and point out that even though the lowercase form does connect, the uppercase letter does not connect to the lowercase letters that follow it.

59

Guided Practice

Guide the completion of worktext page 47—Tell the students to compare the PreCursive and cursive letters. Point out that uppercase cursive *o* overlaps at the top and that lowercase *o* begins with the cursive stroke. Instruct the class to trace the gray and dotted line guides while you repeat the formation of the strokes of each letter. Encourage the class to write the line of double *o*s with extra care.

Optional Activity

Direct an alphabet identification activity—Allow the students to browse through old magazines to find pictures that start with the letter *o*. Allow them to make a giant collage of the pictures on a big outline that you have prepared on butcher paper or cardboard cut in an *o* shape as the background.

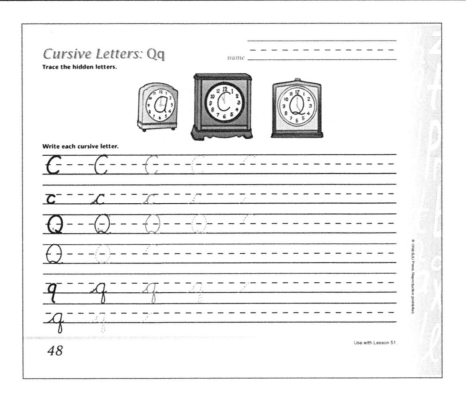

Materials and Preparation

Prepare:

- Separate flashcards with uppercase and lowercase *a, c,* and *o* written on them in cursive, making six cards in all. Secretly attach them to various objects in the classroom.

- Handwriting lines on the chalkboard.

- The following words in PreCursive on the chalkboard.

     quick   *quill*   *Queen Anne's lace*

——— Lesson Content ———

Introduction

Generate interest with a game—Play "I'm Going on a Letter Hunt" (to the rhythm of "I'm Going on a Bear Hunt"). The students echo the teacher's words and rhythm.

   Teacher: We're going on a letter hunt.
   Students: We're going on a letter hunt.
   Teacher: We're going on a letter hunt.
   Students: We're going on a letter hunt.
   Teacher: We know how to write.
   Students: We know how to write.
   Teacher: So, we're going on a letter hunt.
   Students: So, we're going on a letter hunt.
   Teacher: Don't forget your pencil.
   Students: Don't forget your pencil.
   Teacher: Don't forget your paper.
   Students: Don't forget your paper.

   Teacher: 'Cause we're going on a letter hunt!
   Students: 'Cause we're going on a letter hunt!

Then explain to the students that six flashcards with cursive letters have been hidden in the room. They cannot leave their desks to find them, but if a student sees one from where he is, he may raise his hand and tell where he sees it. Each student who is first to find a flashcard may write the letter in PreCursive on the chalkboard.

Skill Development

Demonstrate the formation of uppercase and lowercase cursive *q*—Verbalize the direction of the strokes as you write each letter on the chalkboard. Compare cursive *q* to PreCursive *q*.

(1) Begin at one,
    Swing around to lock.
(2) Curve and slash.

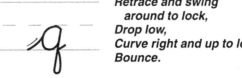

Swing up and around to one,
Retrace and swing
    around to lock,
Drop low,
Curve right and up to lock,
Bounce.

Demonstrate the connecting of the letters in words—Choose a student to read the words on the chalkboard. Then write the words in cursive and point out that both the uppercase and lowercase *q* connect to the lowercase letters that follow them.

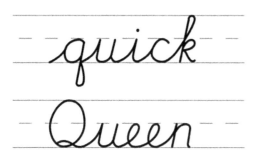

Guide the completion of worktext page 48—Choose a student to read the first line of instructions. Allow time for the students to find the hidden letters. Review the formation of cursive *c* and verbalize the direction of the stroke for cursive *q*, noting the difference between the cursive and PreCursive forms. As the students complete the page, check on their posture, paper position, pencil hold, and letter formation.

Optional Activity

Direct a writing and art activity—Tell the students to draw a picture of a bear hunt. Instruct them to hide letters in the drawing. Let them exchange papers with a friend and discover the hidden letters.

Materials and Preparation

Have available:

- The flashcards for each uppercase and lowercase cursive *a*, *c*, and *o*.

Prepare:

- A flashcard for *q*.
- Handwriting lines on the chalkboard.
- The following words in PreCursive on the chalkboard.

        guess   rug   George

—— Lesson Content ——

Introduction

Lead a rhythm activity—Invite the children to join in the rhythm activity, "I'm Going on a Letter Hunt," from the previous lesson. After repeating the words, direct four students to stand in front of the class with their eyes closed, facing the chalkboard. Give eight other students the letter flashcards prepared earlier and tell them to hide the cards behind themselves. Then instruct the rest of the class to join in the game by pretending to hide a card behind themselves. Tell the four students in front of the class to turn around and choose a classmate they believe is holding a card. If the student guessing is correct, he may write the cursive letter on the chalkboard. If any of the children who were originally holding the flashcards have not been chosen by the end of the game, they may write the letter on the chalkboard.

Skill Development

Demonstrate the formation of uppercase and lowercase cursive *g*—Verbalize the direction of the strokes as you write each letter on the chalkboard.

Begin at one,
Swing around to three,
Drop low and loop.

Swing up and around
* to one,*
Retrace and swing
* around to lock,*
Drop low and loop.

Demonstrate the writing of the lowercase *g* in pairs—Point out that the pencil is not lifted between the letters. Instruct the class to air-trace the letter *g* in pairs and then have several students practice writing the letter in pairs on the chalkboard.

Demonstrate the connecting of the letters in words—Instruct a student to read the words on the chalkboard. Then write the words in cursive writing and point out that both the uppercase and lowercase *g* connect to the lowercase letters that follow them.

Guided Practice

Guide the completion of worktext page 49—Discuss the difference between cursive and PreCursive *g*. As the students trace the gray and dotted line guides, repeat the direction of each stroke. Take the Timothy Time puppet on a walk around the classroom to check the formation of the pairs of *g*s on the bottom line.

Optional Activity

Direct the writing of letters in pairs—Distribute handwriting paper and instruct the class to write five pairs of each of the following letters: *a, o, c,* and *g*. Remind them to space correctly between each pair of letters.

Lesson 53   Cursive Letters: *Ee*   Worktext page 50

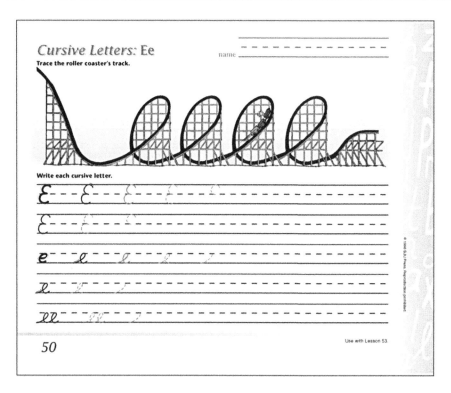

Materials and Preparation

Prepare:

- Handwriting lines on the chalkboard.
- The following words in PreCursive on the chalkboard.

    deed   *Ellen*   *eye*

———— Lesson Content ————

Introduction

Read the poem "Writing Time" in unison.

> See Lesson 47 for the poem "Writing Time."

Skill Development

Demonstrate the formation of uppercase and lowercase cursive *e*—Verbalize the direction of the strokes as you write each letter on the chalkboard. Point out that the formation of the PreCursive and cursive uppercase *e* is the same.

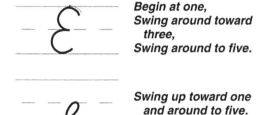

Begin at one,
Swing around toward
   three,
Swing around to five.

Swing up toward one
   and around to five.

Demonstrate the writing of lowercase *e* in pairs.

Demonstrate the connecting of the letters in words—Instruct a student to read the words on the chalkboard. Then write the words in cursive writing and point out that both the uppercase and lowercase *e* connect to the lowercase letters that follow them.

Guided Practice

Guide the completion of worktext page 50—Instruct the students to finger-trace Timothy Time's ride. Choose a volunteer to read the directions. Tell the students to trace the gray and dotted line guides. Draw attention to the pairs of *es* on the bottom line. Tell the class to take extra care in spacing the *es* correctly.

Optional Activity

Direct an alphabetizing activity—Scramble and write the lowercase letters *a, c, e, g,* and *o* on the chalkboard in PreCursive. Instruct the students to number their handwriting paper from 1 to 5 and then to write the letters in alphabetical order using cursive handwriting. Beside each lowercase letter have them write the corresponding uppercase cursive letter three times.

Lesson 54	Time to Practice	Worktext page 51

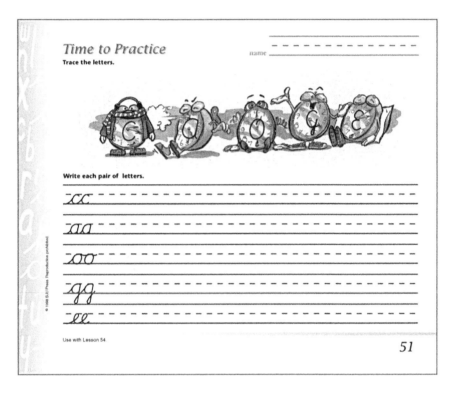

Materials and Preparation

Prepare:

• The following words in cursive on the chalkboard.

| Oliver | look | boat | shoe |
| Ed | toy | Gail | coat |

———— Lesson Content ————

Introduction

Generate interest with animated letters—Direct the students to identify the clocks at the top of worktext page 51 as they follow these directions:

1. Draw a Quiet Clock next to Gabby Clock.
2. Draw ice cubes around Cold Clock.
3. Draw two more springs on broken Overworked Clock.

4. Draw a handkerchief for sneezy Allergic Clock.
5. Draw another pillow for sleepy Exhausted Clock to rest on.

Skill Development

Review the connecting of letters—Draw attention to the cursive words written on the chalkboard. Point out that the uppercase *o* does not connect to lowercase letters and that the beginning of the stroke for the next letter starts close to the uppercase letter but does not touch it. Emphasize the connecting stroke that sweeps out of the lowercase *o*.

Guided Practice

Direct the completion of worktext page 51—Instruct the students to finger-trace the letters inside the animated clocks

as you verbalize the direction of the strokes. Tell the students to complete the page independently.

Optional Activity

Direct a writing and art activity—Encourage the students to design and label two or three other clock characters for the letters *a, c, e, g,* and *o.*

Lesson 55   Time to Ring (an assessment)   Worktext page 52

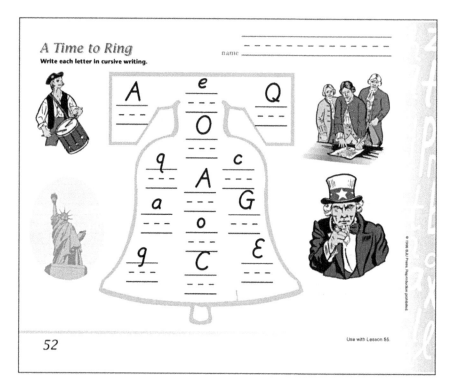

Materials and Preparation

No materials or prelesson preparation is needed for this lesson.

——— Lesson Content ———

Introduction

Generate interest with patriotic pictures—Direct a student to read the title of worktext page 52. Instruct the class to note the silhouette of the Liberty Bell. Discuss the four background pictures by asking:

➤ What instrument is the boy playing in the picture at the top of the page on the left? *(drum)* Has anyone ever seen a drummer in a parade?

➤ What are the men doing in the picture at the top on the right side? *(signing the Declaration of Independence)* Is the signing of the Declaration of Inde-

pendence an important part of history? *(yes)* Was it a day on which to ring the Liberty Bell? *(yes)*

➤ What is the name of the statue at the bottom on the left side? *(Statue of Liberty)* Has anyone visited the Statue of Liberty?

➤ Who is the man at the bottom of the page on the right? *(Uncle Sam)* Is he a real person? *(no)* What does he make you think of?

Assessment

Direct the completion of worktext page 52—Tell a student to read the directions. Instruct the students to write the cursive letters on the lines below the PreCursive letters. Tell the class to use their best writing as they complete the activity independently.

Optional Activity

Direct a writing activity—Write the following sentences on the chalkboard in cursive. Instruct the students to write them in PreCursive on handwriting paper.

The historic Liberty Bell was made in England.

The inscription on the Liberty Bell is taken from Leviticus 25:10. "Proclaim liberty throughout all the land unto all the inhabitants thereof."

Lesson 56	Cursive Letters: *Ii*	Worktext page 53

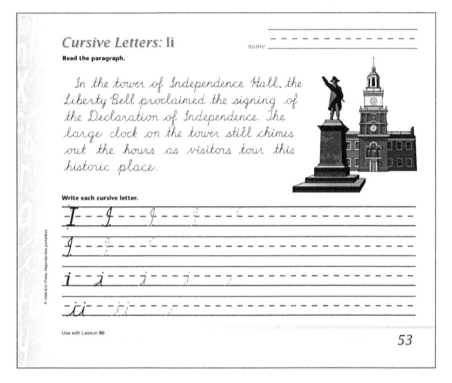

Materials and Preparation

Prepare:

- Handwriting lines on the chalkboard.
- The following words in PreCursive on the chalkboard.

   Indian   icicle   smile

Lesson Content

Introduction

Sing "The Handwriting Song."

Skill Development

Demonstrate the formation of uppercase and lowercase cursive *i*—Verbalize the direction of the strokes as you write each letter on the chalkboard. Compare cursive *i* with Pre-Cursive *i*.

Swing around and up,
Drop and swing left,
Retrace and sweep up.

Swing up,
Drop and curve.
Dot.

Demonstrate the writing of lowercase *i* in pairs.

Demonstrate the connecting of the letters in words—Instruct a student to read the words on the chalkboard. Then write the words in cursive and point out that both the uppercase and lowercase *i* connect to the lowercase letters that follow them.

Guided Practice

Direct the completion of worktext page 53—Read the paragraph at the top of the page to the class. Discuss the word *independence* and its meaning of self-government. Emphasize the great heritage that Americans have. Instruct the students to complete the page independently.

Optional Activity

Direct an alphabetizing activity—Tell the students to alphabetize the each group of uppercase letters, using cursive writing.

1. O A Q G
2. E A I C
3. C A O I
4. I G Q E
5. G E A I

Lesson 57   Cursive Letters: *Jj*   Worktext page 54

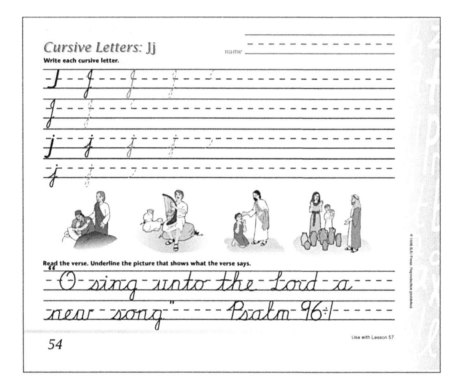

Materials and Preparation

Prepare:

- Handwriting lines on the chalkboard.
- The following words in PreCursive on the chalkboard.

    Jill   *jelly*   *subject*   *rejoice*

——— Lesson Content ———

Introduction

Read the poem "Writing Time"—Use the Timothy Time puppet to pantomime the words.

Skill Development

Review the formation of uppercase and lowercase cursive *i*.

Demonstrate the formation of uppercase and lowercase cursive *j*—Verbalize the direction of the strokes as you write each letter on the chalkboard. Allow several children to write the letters on the chalkboard as you verbalize the strokes several more times.

Swing around and up,
Drop low and loop.

68

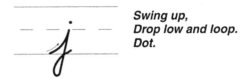

Swing up,
Drop low and loop.
Dot.

Demonstrate the connecting of the letters in words—Instruct a student to read the words on the chalkboard. Write the words in cursive and point out that both the uppercase and lowercase *j* connect to the lowercase letters that follow them.

Jill

Guided Practice

Guide the completion of worktext page 54—Repeat the strokes as the students trace the gray and dotted line guides. Tell the children to complete the top four lines. Choose a volunteer to read the second line of instructions. Give the students time to complete the exercise; then check the answers as a class.

Optional Activity

Direct a writing activity—Instruct the students to write this quotation from Nehemiah 8:10 in PreCursive on handwriting paper:

"The joy of the Lord is your strength."

Lesson 58   Travels (a review)

Materials and Preparation

Prepare:

- The following columns of words on the chalkboard, the first column in cursive and the second in PreCursive.

Iowa	*Massachusetts*
Georgia	*Iowa*
Hawaii	*California*
Massachusetts	*Georgia*
California	*Hawaii*

- Handwriting lines on the chalkboard.

———— Lesson Content ————

Introduction

Generate interest with a matching game—Read the names of the states on the chalkboard. Choose volunteers to draw a line to match the pairs of state names on the chalkboard. Point out the similarities between the cursive and PreCursive letters.

Skill Development

Review the formation of uppercase and lowercase *c*, *a*, *o*, *q*, *g*, *e*, *i*, and *j*—Verbalize the direction of the strokes as you write each letter on the chalkboard.

Guided Practice

Guide a traveling game—Tell the students to write the sentence *Quincy is taking a trip to the Arctic.* in PreCursive at the top of their handwriting paper. Instruct the students to complete the activity by listing in PreCursive the objects Quincy will take with him. The names of these objects must begin with the review letters *c*, *o*, *a*, *q*, *g*, *e*, *i*, or *j*. After each object is written, direct the students to write the first letter of the word in cursive.

Optional Activity

Direct a composing activity—Encourage the students to write about traveling they have done and the things they took with them. Instruct them to use PreCursive handwriting.

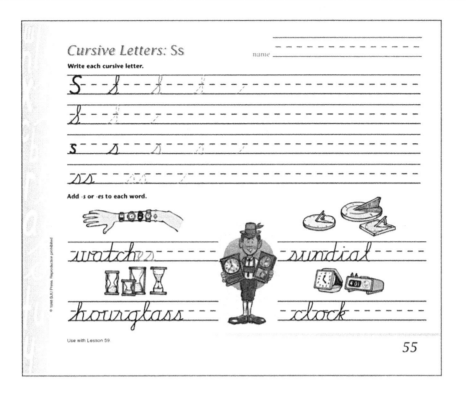

Materials and Preparation

Have available:

• The Timothy Time puppet.

Prepare:

• The following words on the chalkboard in cursive.

wristwatch	sundial	hourglass
cuckoo clock	stopwatch	alarm clock

• The following words on the chalkboard in PreCursive.

sister	frost	Sharon	class

Lesson Content

Introduction

Create interest in today's lesson—Using the Timothy Time puppet, invite the children to join Timothy Time in his uncle's clock shop. Tell them that Timothy Time will pretend to read the names of some of the types of clocks found in his uncle's shop. Then have Timothy Time tell how many of each type of clock his uncle has on the shelves. First, have Timothy Time pretend to count out five wristwatches. Ask a student to write the numeral *5* in front of the word *wristwatch*. Read the numeral and the word *wristwatch* as it is without the correct plural ending. Ask the class what is missing. As they supply the *-es* ending, write it in correctly. Continue through the list, allowing the children to write the numerals Timothy Time tells them as you add the *-s* or *-es*.

Skill Development

Demonstrate the formation of uppercase and lowercase cursive *s*—Verbalize the direction of the strokes as you write each letter on the chalkboard. Compare cursive *s* to PreCursive *s*. Point out that uppercase PreCursive is visible in uppercase cursive *s* and that lowercase *s* is half of uppercase cursive *s*.

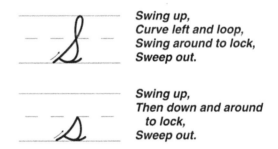

Swing up,
Curve left and loop,
Swing around to lock,
Sweep out.

Swing up,
Then down and around
  to lock,
Sweep out.

Demonstrate the writing of lowercase *s* in pairs.

Demonstrate the connecting of the letters in words—Instruct a student to read the words on the chalkboard. Then write the words in cursive and point out that both the uppercase and lowercase *s* connect to the lowercase letters that follow them.

Guided Practice

Guide the completion of worktext page 55—Repeat the direction of each stroke as the students trace the gray and dotted line guides. Tell the students to complete the top four lines. Check their work as you move around the classroom.

Choose a student to read the next sentence of directions. Read the first example aloud saying, "One watch, two—." Point out that *watches* has an -*es* on the end. Instruct the students to fill in the blanks. Continue with the other three examples.

Optional Activity

Direct composing of words—Write the cursive letters *c, a, o, q, g, e, i, j,* and *s* on the chalkboard. Distribute handwriting paper and challenge the students to see who can make the most words from these letters.

Lesson 60   Cursive Letters: *Dd*   Worktext page 56

Cursive Letters: Dd   name

Write each cursive letter.

D

D

d

dd

Write each sentence.

Sadie aids Dad

Sadie is a good dog

56   Use with Lesson 60

Materials and Preparation

Have available:

- The poem "Writing Time" on chart paper.

Prepare:

- The following words in PreCursive on the chalkboard.

    duck   puddle   food   Dana

- Handwriting lines on the chalkboard.

———— Lesson Content ————

Introduction

Create interest in today's lesson—Use the Timothy Time puppet to pretend to read the poem "Writing Time" to the class. Let him call on students to come to the chart to point out words with the letter *d* in them.

Skill Development

Demonstrate the formation of uppercase and lowercase cursive *d*—Verbalize the direction of the strokes as you write each letter on the chalkboard. Compare cursive and PreCursive *d*.

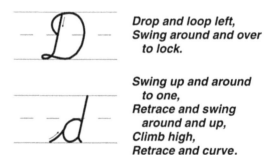

Drop and loop left,
Swing around and over
  to lock.

Swing up and around
  to one,
Retrace and swing
  around and up,
Climb high,
Retrace and curve.

Demonstrate the writing of lowercase *d* in pairs.

Demonstrate the connecting of the letters in words—Instruct a student to read the words on the chalkboard. Then write the words in cursive and point out that the uppercase letter *d* does not connect to the lowercase letters that follow it.

72

Guided Practice

Guide the completion of worktext page 56—Tell the students to trace the gray and dotted line guides as you verbalize each stroke. Choose a volunteer to read the next line of directions. Allow two students to read the sentences. Instruct the class to complete the activity, encouraging them to use their best cursive handwriting.

Optional Activity

Direct a writing activity—Encourage the students to write and illustrate the funny questions below.

1. Is Eddie's dog sad?
2. Did Ed's eel jog?
3. Does Sadie dodge geese?

Lesson 61   Matching (a review)   Worktext page 57

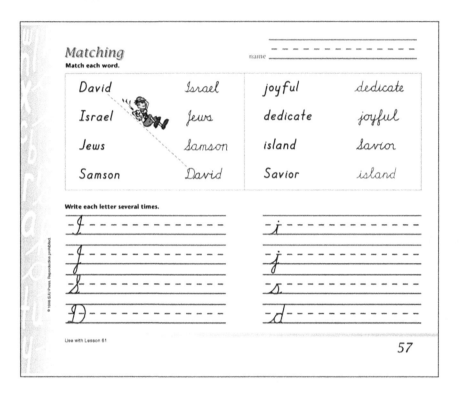

Materials and Preparation

Prepare:

• Handwriting lines on the chalkboard.

—————— Lesson Content ——————

Introduction

Sing "The Handwriting Song"—Allow a student to lead the song using the Timothy Time puppet.

Skill Development

Review the formation of uppercase and lowercase *i, j, s,* and *d*—Point out that all of these letters are written in one continuous stroke. Verbalize the direction of each stroke as

students demonstrate the letter formations on the chalkboard.

Guided Practice

Guide the completion of worktext page 57—Choose a volunteer to read the directions. Check the matching section as you walk around the classroom. Remind the students to space correctly as they write each letter four times.

Optional Activity

Direct a matching activity—Help the students make a separate flashcard for each cursive and PreCursive uppercase and lowercase *c, a, o, q, g, e, i, j, s,* and *d.* Let them practice matching the cursive and PreCursive cards as they time themselves.

Materials and Preparation

Prepare:

- The following names in cursive on the chalkboard.

  Daniel   Samuel   Joseph   Delilah
  Isaac   Jonah   Solomon   Israel

- Handwriting lines on the chalkboard.

———— Lesson Content ————

Introduction

Generate interest with a Bible activity—Ask the children what initials are. Direct attention to the Bible names on the chalkboard. Read the clues below, allowing students to raise their hands if they know which name matches the clue. If a student answers correctly, he may go to the chalkboard and write the initial of that man or woman on the handwriting lines. As he writes the initial, verbalize the direction of each stroke to help reinforce proper writing formation. Check for correct punctuation and slant.

1. The king had to cast him into the lion's den. *(Daniel)*
2. He thought Eli called him one night, but it was the Lord. *(Samuel)*
3. He had a coat of many colors. *(Joseph)*
4. She tricked Samson into telling where his strength came from. *(Delilah)*
5. Abraham offered him as a sacrifice, but the Lord sent a ram to take his place. *(Isaac)*
6. He was swallowed by a great fish. *(Jonah)*
7. This son of David became a wise king. *(Solomon)*
8. His name had been Jacob. The nation of the Jews is still called by the new name God gave him. *(Israel)*

Assessment

Direct the completion of worktext page 58—Choose a volunteer to read the instructions and the name of each Bible character. Read Psalm 46:1 and then lead the class in reading it in unison. Point out that the sentence is to be written two times. Remind the class to do their best as they complete the activities. Collect papers and evaluate.

Optional Activity

Direct the writing of letters in pairs—Distribute handwriting paper and instruct the students to write five pairs of each lowercase *g, i, e, s,* and *d.*

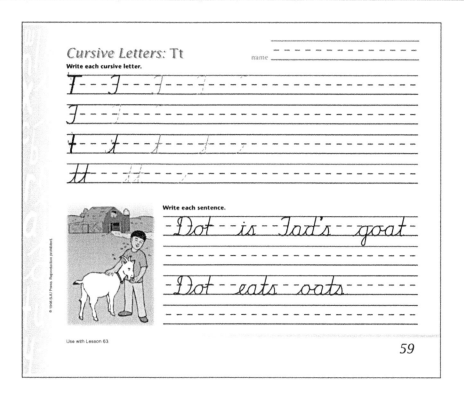

Materials and Preparation

Prepare:

- Handwriting lines on the chalkboard.
- The following words in PreCursive on the chalkboard.

  mitten   tot   toad   Todd

——— Lesson Content ———

Introduction

Create interest in today's lesson—Write a cursive letter *t* on the chalkboard. Encourage students to name objects in the classroom that begin with the letter *t*. Write the objects on the chalkboard as students suggest them.

Skill Development

Demonstrate the formation of uppercase and lowercase cursive *t*—Verbalize the direction of the strokes as you write each letter on the chalkboard. Direct the class to air-trace the letters and then allow several students to practice writing the letters on the chalkboard.

**Swing over and up,
Drop and swing left.**

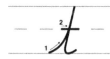

**(1) Swing up,
Retrace and curve.
(2) Cross.**

Demonstrate the writing of lowercase *t* in pairs.

Demonstrate the connecting of the letters in words—Instruct a student to read the words on the chalkboard. Then write the words in cursive and point out that the uppercase *t* does not connect to the lowercase letters that follow it. Allow several students to practice writing the words *mitten, tot, toad,* and *Todd* on the chalkboard.

Guided Practice

Direct the completion of worktext page 59—Instruct the students to read the directions and to complete the activity independently.

Optional Activity

Direct a writing and art activity—Instruct the students to fold their handwriting paper into fourths and illustrate the following groups of words, one in each section. Tell them to label each illustration using their best cursive writing.

Stacie's coat	*good dog*
sad cat	*Dad eats.*

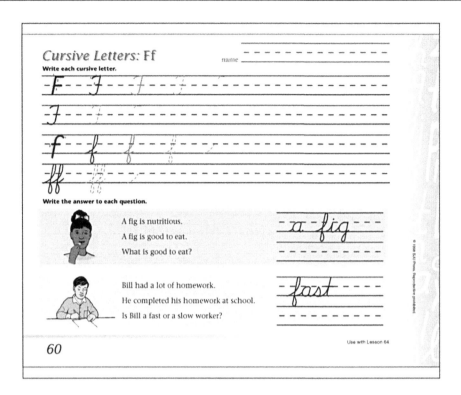

Materials and Preparation

Prepare:

- The following words in PreCursive on the chalkboard.

  tuff   Fido   off

- Handwriting lines on the chalkboard.

———— Lesson Content ————

Introduction

Play a guessing game—Encourage the students to guess the new cursive letter to be learned by allowing them to ask questions such as *Is the new letter one of the letters in* town? or *Is it the last letter in* funny?

Skill Development

Review the formation of uppercase and lowercase cursive *t*.

Demonstrate the formation of uppercase and lowercase cursive *f*—Verbalize the direction of the strokes as you write each letter on the chalkboard. Point out the similarity of uppercase *t* and *f*. Lead the class as they air-trace the letters and practice writing them on the chalkboard.

**(1) Swing over and up,
    Drop and swing left.**
(2) Cross.

*Swing up,
Curve left and drop low,
Curve right and up to lock,
Bounce.*

Demonstrate the writing of lowercase *f* in pairs.

Demonstrate the connecting of the letters in words—Instruct a student to read the words on the chalkboard. Then write the words in cursive and point out that the uppercase *f* does not connect to the lowercase letters that follow it. Call attention to the way the letters *o* and *f* connect in the word *off*. Allow several students to practice writing the words in cursive handwriting on the chalkboard.

Guided Practice

Guide the completion of worktext page 60—Choose a volunteer to read the instructions for both activities. Tell the students to complete the work independently.

Optional Activity

Direct a writing activity—Instruct the students to write the following words in cursive on handwriting paper. Tell them to underline the words that have a long vowel sound.

1.	*fad*	*fed*	*fade*
2.	*gate*	*got*	*get*
3.	*Dale*	*deed*	*dog*
4.	*tale*	*toad*	*tot*
5.	*Sid*	*site*	*sit*

Lesson 65   Lists (a review)

Materials and Preparation

Have available:

- Handwriting paper for each student.

Prepare:

- The following list of words on the chalkboard.

    eggs   dates   cocoa   oats   tea   catfood

- Handwriting lines on the chalkboard.

———— Lesson Content ————

Introduction

Generate interest in today's lesson—Direct attention to the list of words written on the chalkboard. Ask the students if the list reminds them of their mother's grocery list. Discuss the purpose of other types of lists students may have seen or used.

Skill Development

Review the formation of uppercase and lowercase *t* and *f*—Verbalize the direction of the strokes as you write each letter on the chalkboard. Allow several students to write the letters on the chalkboard.

Guided Practice

Direct writing on handwriting paper—Tell the students to write the grocery list from the chalkboard on the handwriting paper. Instruct them to use their best cursive writing.

Optional Activity

Direct a composing activity—Distribute handwriting paper and instruct the students to list the activities they will do when they get home from school. Tell them to write in PreCursive.

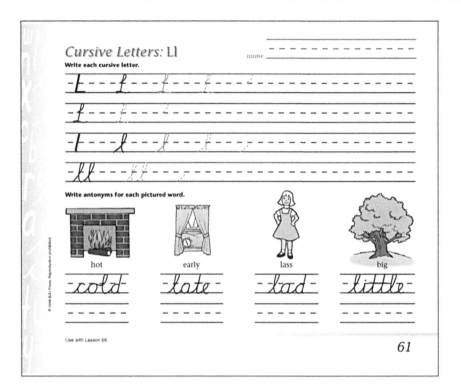

Materials and Preparation

Prepare:

- The following list in cursive on the chalkboard.

high	early	lad
long	lass	low
dark	big	light
lady	short	cry
laugh	gentleman	late
hot	cold	little

- The words *bell, laddie, lift,* and *sell* in PreCursive on the chalkboard.
- Handwriting lines on the chalkboard.

——— Lesson Content ———

Introduction

Sing "The Handwriting Song."

Create interest in today's lesson—Direct attention to the lists on the chalkboard. Allow several students to draw lines to match the antonyms.

Skill Development

Demonstrate the formation of uppercase and lowercase cursive *l*—Verbalize the direction of the strokes as you write each letter on the chalkboard. Tell the students to compare the PreCursive and cursive models. Then choose volunteers to practice writing the letters on the chalkboard.

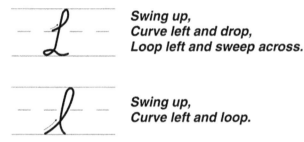

Swing up,
Curve left and drop,
Loop left and sweep across.

Swing up,
Curve left and loop.

Demonstrate the writing of lowercase *l* in pairs.

Demonstrate the connecting of the letters in words—Direct a student to read the second list of words on the chalkboard. Then write the words in cursive and point out that both the uppercase and lowercase *l* connect to the lowercase letters that follow them. Allow several students to practice writing the words on the chalkboard.

Guided Practice

Guide the completion of worktext page 61—Choose a student to read the directions for both activities. As the class completes the page independently, circulate among the students and observe their posture, paper position, and pencil hold.

Optional Activity

Direct a writing activity—Tell the students to write the words below in cursive and to write antonyms for each word in PreCursive.

fat	lift	less
lie	soft	go

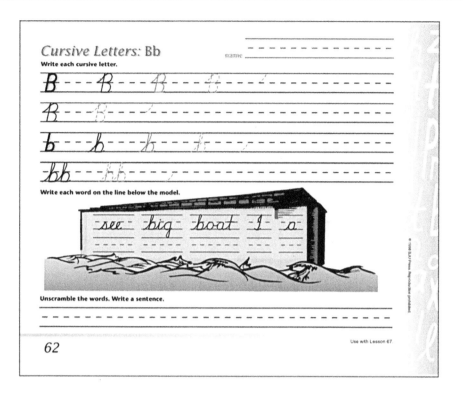

Cursive Letters: Bb   name
Write each cursive letter.

Write each word on the line below the model.

see   big   boat   I   a

Unscramble the words. Write a sentence.

62   Use with Lesson 67.

Materials and Preparation

Prepare:

- The following words in PreCursive on the chalkboard.

  Bob   babble   bird   Bible

- Handwriting lines on the chalkboard.

———— Lesson Content ————

Introduction

Create interest in today's lesson—Read the biblical account of the Flood from Genesis 7:13-17 to the students.

Skill Development

Demonstrate the formation of uppercase and lowercase cursive *b*—Verbalize the direction of the strokes as you write each letter on the chalkboard. Point out that lowercase PreCursive *b* is visible in cursive *b*. Let two children at a time come to the chalkboard to write the letters as you verbalize the strokes again.

**Swing up and drop,
Retrace and swing
   around to lock,
Retrace and swing
   around to lock,
Sweep out.**

**Swing up,
Curve left and drop,
Retrace and swing
   around to lock,
Sweep out.**

Demonstrate the writing of lowercase *b* in pairs.

Demonstrate the connecting of the letters in words—Instruct a student to read the words on the chalkboard. Then write the words in cursive and point out that both the uppercase and lowercase *b* connect to the lowercase letters that follow them. Allow time for several students to practice writing the letters on the chalkboard. Make sure the letter *b* is locked on the baseline.

Guided Practice

Guide the completion of worktext page 62—Allow a volunteer to read the first sentence of the directions. After the students have completed the top four lines, read the next two sentences of directions. Unscramble the words together.

Optional Activity

Direct an art and writing activity—Tell the students to write the following sentence in PreCursive and illustrate it: *God set a rainbow over the earth at the end of the flood.*

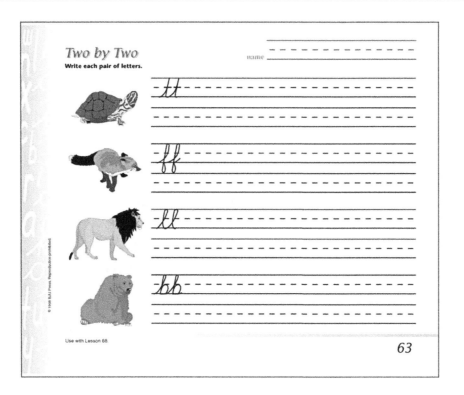

Materials and Preparation

Prepare:

- The cursive letters *t, f, l,* and *b* on the chalkboard.
- Handwriting lines on the chalkboard.

——— Lesson Content ———

Introduction

Create interest in today's lesson—Direct the students' attention to the letters on the chalkboard. Tell various students to dictate animal names that begin with those letters. Write each name in cursive on the chalkboard.

Skill Development

Review the formation of uppercase and lowercase *t, f, l,* and *b*—Verbalize the direction of the strokes as you write each letter on the chalkboard. Allow several students to write the lowercase letters in pairs on the chalkboard.

Guided Practice

Guide the completion of worktext page 63—Choose a volunteer to read the directions. Verbalize the letter formations as the students finger-trace the models. Allow the class to complete the page independently.

Optional Activity

Direct a writing activity—Write the following words and sentences in cursive on the chalkboard:

leaf   floated   God   flood   beasts

1. God sent a great ___.
2. God sent the ___ two by two.
3. The door of the ark was shut by ____.
4. The ark ___ on the water.
5. The dove brought back an olive ___.

Tell the students to number their papers from one to five. Instruct them to read each sentence and then to write the correct word for the blank beside the number on their paper.

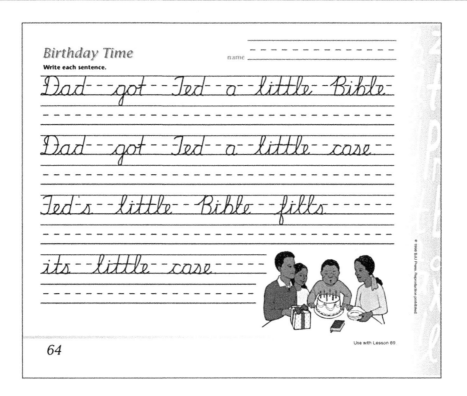

Materials and Preparation

Have available:

- The chart with the poem "Writing Time." (See Lesson 7)

Prepare:

- The following sentence in cursive on the chalkboard. Use inconsistent slant.

Jeff's best gift is a little Bible.

——— Lesson Content ———

Introduction

Create interest with a poem—Lead the students in reading the poem "Writing Time" in unison. Point out that all the letters are leaning in the same direction. Choose a volunteer to read the line from the poem that tells them to use the correct slant when writing.

Skill Development

Review correct slanting—Direct the students' attention to the sentence written on the chalkboard. Allow several stu-

dents to erase the letters that are not slanted correctly; then let them write again, using correct slant.

Assessment

Direct the completion of worktext page 64—Choose a student to read the instructions and the sentences to be written. Remind them to slant each letter correctly.

Optional Activity

Direct a writing activity—Write the following verses in cursive on the chalkboard. Tell the students to number their papers from one to six. Instruct them to locate the following verses in their Bibles and then to write the words that belong in the blanks next to the correct number.

Romans 6:23: "But the (1) of (2) is eternal (3) through Jesus Christ our Lord."

James 1:17: "Every (4)   (5) and every perfect (6) is from above, and cometh down from the Father of lights."

Cursive Letters: Hh   name

Write each cursive letter.

H - H - H

h - h - h

h

Write each sentence.

Hal held the flag.

He held it at school.

He held it high.

Use with Lesson 70

65

Materials and Preparation

Prepare:

- Handwriting lines on the chalkboard.
- This sentence in PreCursive on the chalkboard.

   Hal and Henry held Harry's helmet.

——— Lesson Content ———

Introduction

Sing "The Handwriting Song."

Skill Development

Demonstrate the formation of uppercase and lowercase cursive *h*—Verbalize the direction of the strokes as you write each letter on the chalkboard. Point out that the Pre-Cursive letter is visible in the cursive letter. Explain that it is an honor both to hold the flag and to say the pledge to it. Write the word *honor* on the chalkboard. Direct the child who held the flag or led the pledge to write the letter *h* on the chalkboard as you describe it.

(1) Swing up and drop.
(2) Drop and climb left,
     Then glide right.

Swing up,
Curve left and drop,
Retrace and swing right,
Drop and curve.

Demonstrate the writing of lowercase *h* in pairs.

Demonstrate the connecting of the letters in words—Instruct a student to read the sentence on the chalkboard. Then write the sentence in cursive and point out that the uppercase letter *h* does not connect to the lowercase letters that follow it.

Guided Practice

Guide the completion of worktext page 65—Direct a student to read the instructions and the sentences. Repeat the stroke directions as the class traces the gray and dotted models. Remind the students to use their best cursive writing as they complete the activities.

Optional Activity

Direct an art activity—Allow the students to draw and color a Christian flag on construction paper.

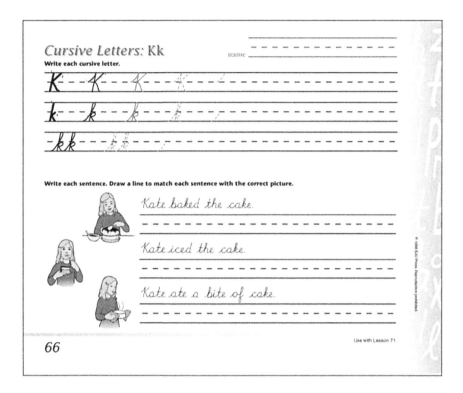

Materials and Preparation

Prepare:

- Handwriting lines on the chalkboard.
- These sentences in cursive on the chalkboard.

> *Kile built the plane.*
>
> *Kile bought the model plane.*
>
> *Kile painted the plane.*

———— Lesson Content ————

Introduction

Direct a sequencing activity—Direct attention to the chalkboard. Choose a student to read the sentences. Ask if Kile could have built the plane before he bought it. Instruct a volunteer to number the sentences in the correct order. Direct another student to read the sentences in the right order.

Skill Development

Demonstrate the formation of uppercase and lowercase cursive *k*—Verbalize the direction of the strokes as you write each letter on the chalkboard. Point out that the Pre-Cursive letter is visible in the cursive letter.

(1) Swing up and drop.
(2) Drop left,
Then right and curve.

Swing up,
Curve left and drop,
Retrace and swing
   around to lock,
Drop right to curve.

Demonstrate the writing of lowercase *k* in pairs.

Demonstrate the connecting of the letters in words—Using cursive, write the sentence *Kile can make the plane fly high.* on the chalkboard. Point out that both the uppercase and lowercase *k* connect to the lowercase letters that follow them.

Guided Practice

Guide the completion of worktext page 66—Direct a student to read the instructions and the sentences. Repeat the stroke directions as the class traces the gray and dotted models. Remind the students to use their best cursive writing as they complete the activities.

Optional Activity

Direct a handwriting activity—Instruct the students to sequence and write the following sentences in cursive on handwriting paper:

> *Keith skated at the lake.*
> *Keith tied his skates.*
> *Keith took off his boots.*

Lesson 72　　　　　　　　A Review

Materials and Preparation

Have available:

- Handwriting paper for each student.

Prepare:

- Handwriting lines on the chalkboard.
- The following paragraph in cursive on the chalkboard.

Hal kicked Kit's ball. He kicked it high! He had to chase the ball. At last he got it.

——— Lesson Content ———

Introduction

Create interest in today's lesson—Intruct five students to pretend to be words in a sentence. Tell them to demonstrate correct spacing of words by standing at equal distances from each other. Then tell them to vary the distances. Select other students to position them correctly.

Skill Development

Review the formation of uppercase and lowercase *h* and *k*—Verbalize the direction of the strokes as you write each letter on the chalkboard. Direct attention to the paragraph on the chalkboard. Choose a child to identify the uppercase letter that does not connect to lowercase letters (H), and the uppercase letters that do connect to lowercase letters (A and K).

Guided Practice

Direct the writing of a paragraph—Instruct the students to write the paragraph from the chalkboard on handwriting paper. Remind them to space correctly as they write each word.

Optional Activity

Direct writing of a recipe—Write the recipe for gladness on chart paper or on the chalkboard. Instruct the students to write the recipe on handwriting paper.

To Be Glad

1. basket of delight
2. kisses to Dad
3. kisses to Sis
4. good deeds

Materials and Preparation

Prepare:

- The following sentence in PreCursive on the chalkboard.

  Nancy is Ned and Nan's niece.

- Handwriting lines on the chalkboard.

——— **Lesson Content** ———

Introduction

Generate interest by leading a hymn—Sing "Praise Him, Praise Him, All Ye Little Children" using the following verse:

> Praise Him, praise Him,
> All ye little children,
> God made us,
> God made us.

Read Psalm 19:14—Point out that as God made each of us with special care, we should glorify Him by performing every task with care. Even our writing should be done with care.

Skill Development

Demonstrate the formation of uppercase and lowercase cursive *n*—Verbalize the direction of the strokes as you write each letter on the chalkboard. Compare the cursive letter *n* with the PreCursive letter *n*. Point out that the cursive stroke has been added to the PreCursive letter. Demonstrate how easily *n* can be written.

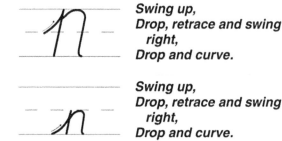

Swing up,
Drop, retrace and swing right,
Drop and curve.

Swing up,
Drop, retrace and swing right,
Drop and curve.

Demonstrate the writing of lowercase *n* in pairs.

Demonstrate the connecting of the letters in words—Choose a student to read the sentence on the chalkboard. Then write the sentence in cursive and point out that both the uppercase and lowercase *n* connect to the lowercase letters that follow them.

Guided Practice

Guide the completion of worktext page 67—Choose a volunteer to read the instructions and the verse. As the students complete the exercises, remind them that their writing should be done with care.

Optional Activity

Direct an art and labeling activity—Encourage the students to draw a lion and label its mane, tail, teeth, and nose.

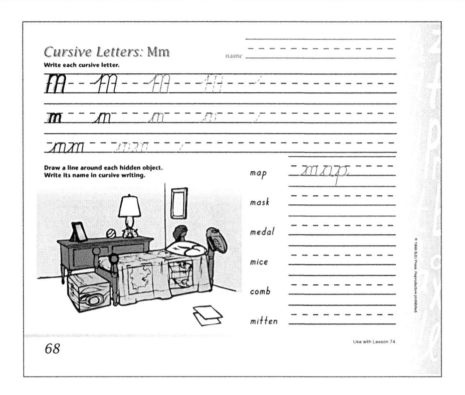

Materials and Preparation

Prepare:

- Handwriting lines on the chalkboard.
- The following letter combinations on the chalkboard using cursive writing, but not connecting the letters.

bca	*gef*	*fde*
gih	*jkl*	*ecd*
hfg	*ikj*	*cbd*

--------- **Lesson Content** ---------

Introduction

Generate interest with an alphabetizing activity—Direct attention to the letters *bca* on the chalkboard. Direct a student to connect the letters as he writes them in alphabetical order. Continue until all the combinations have been written alphabetically.

Skill Development

Review the formation of uppercase and lowercase cursive *n*.

Demonstrate the formation of uppercase and lowercase cursive *m*—Verbalize the direction of the strokes as you write each letter on the chalkboard. Point out that a cursive stroke has been added to the PreCursive letter.

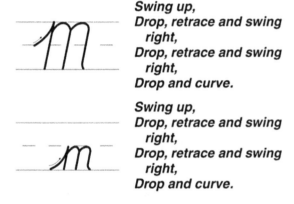

Swing up,
Drop, retrace and swing right,
Drop, retrace and swing right,
Drop and curve.

Swing up,
Drop, retrace and swing right,
Drop, retrace and swing right,
Drop and curve.

Demonstrate the writing of lowercase *m* **in pairs.**

Demonstrate the connecting of the letters in words—Inform the students that the uppercase and lowercase letter *m* connect to the lowercase letters that follow them as you write the sentence *Mack's marshmallows melted.* in cursive.

Guided Practice

Guide the completion of worktext page 68—Choose a volunteer to read the instructions at the top of the page. Repeat the stroke directions as the students trace the gray and dotted models. After the class has completed the first activity, direct a student to read the next set of directions. Circulate among the students to help them find the missing objects.

Direct a writing activity—Write the following letter combinations on the chalkboard. Tell the students to write them in alphabetical order to form words:

eebf	*lem*	*mid*
gbe	*elcl*	*pho*
nfi	*lilh*	*oag*

If time permits, have the students alphabetize the columns of words.

Lesson 75   More Practice   Worktext page 69

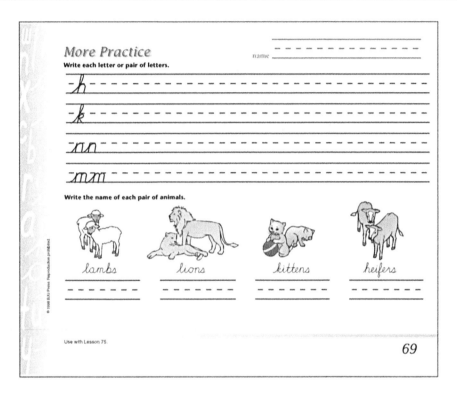

Materials and Preparation

Prepare:

• Handwriting lines on the chalkboard.

——— Lesson Content ———

Introduction

Sing "The Handwriting Song."

Lead a guessing game—Pantomime the formation of *h*. Allow students to guess the letter. Continue the pantomime with *k*, *n*, and *m*. If the students have difficulty in guessing a letter, verbalize each stroke.

Skill Development

Review the formation of uppercase and lowercase *h, k, n,* and *m*—Verbalize the direction of each stroke as students write the letters on the chalkboard.

Review the connecting of the letters in words—Remind the students that uppercase *h* does not connect to the lower-

case letters that follow it. Dictate the following words for students to write on the chalkboard:

cake	*thick*	*make*	*kite*
Kate	*Hal*	*Ned*	*Meg*

Guided Practice

Guide the completion of worktext page 69—Choose a volunteer to read both sets of instructions. Circulate among the students as they complete the page.

Optional Activity

Direct an art and labeling activity—Encourage the students to choose several of the following animals to mold from modeling dough. Tell them to label the animals to make an animal zoo.

koala	*baboon*	*snake*	*moose*	*duck*	*mole*
mouse	*seal*	*lion*	*eagle*	*camel*	*toad*

Materials and Preparation

Have available:

- A picture of a ball game taken from a magazine or newspaper.
- Chart paper and a marker.
- Handwriting paper for each student.

——— Lesson Content ———

Introduction

Generate interest with a picture—Display the picture of a ball game. Discuss what is happening in the picture. As students suggest sentences, write them in paragraph form on the chart paper. Then read the paragraph in unison and choose a title.

Skill Development

Review paragraph structure—Point out the indentation of the first line in the paragraph the class wrote. Ask the class to name the punctuation mark used at the end of each sentence. Point out the space left for margins on both sides of the page.

Assessment

Direct the assessment on worktext page 70—Choose a volunteer to read the directions and the paragraph. Instruct the students to write the paragraph on handwriting paper. Remind them to indent the first line and to leave a margin on both sides of their paper.

Optional Activity

Direct a comprehension activity—Tell the students to refer to worktext page 70 to answer the following questions on handwriting paper:

Whose team beat Mack's team?
Who tossed the ball?
Who hit the ball?
Who slid home?
Whose team lost?

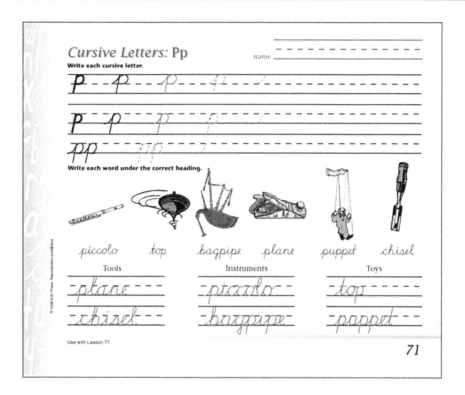

Materials and Preparation

Prepare:

- Handwriting lines on the chalkboard.
- The headings *girls* and *boys* in cursive on the chalkboard.
- The sentence *Penny planted peanuts for Peter.* in Pre-Cursive on the chalkboard.

——— Lesson Content ———

Introduction

Generate interest with a categorizing activity—Point to the headings on the chalkboard while explaining that many things can be put in groups under headings. Tell all the girls to go to the side of the chalkboard with the heading *girls* on it and all the boys to go to the side of the chalkboard with the heading *boys* on it. One by one let them write their names under the correct heading.

Skill Development

Demonstrate the formation of uppercase and lowercase cursive *p*—Verbalize the direction of the strokes as you write each letter on the chalkboard. Allow students who have the letter *p* in their names to write the uppercase and lowercase *p* on the chalkboard.

***Swing up and drop,
Retrace and swing
around to lock.***

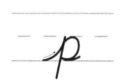

***Swing up,
Drop low,
Retrace and swing
around to lock,
Sweep out.***

Demonstrate the writing of lowercase *p* in pairs.

Demonstrate the connecting of the letters in words—Instruct a student to read the sentence on the chalkboard. Then write the sentence in cursive and point out that the uppercase *p* does not connect to lowercase letters.

Guided Practice

Guide the completion of worktext page 71—Allow a volunteer to read the directions at the top of the page. After the students have completed the first three lines, direct their attention to the bottom of the page. Discuss the pictures, allowing students to name the correct heading for each one. Tell the students to write the words on the writing lines under the correct heading.

Optional Activity

Direct a classifying activity—Tell the students to categorize the list below under the correct headings:

Headings:	*Games*	*Foods*	*Pets*
List:	*apple*	*potato*	*cat*
	tag	*mice*	*hopscotch*
	pickle	*dog*	*hide and seek*

Cursive Letters: Rr   name _____

Write each cursive letter.

R - - R - - R - - R - - - - - -

r - - r - - r - - r - - - - - -

rr - - rr - - - - - - - - - - -

Write the name of each road the train will cross.

Rattle Road

Reel Road

Rooster Road   Roberts Road

Rattle Road   *Rooster Road*

Reel Road   *Roberts Road*

Use with Lesson 78

72

Materials and Preparation

Prepare:

- Handwriting lines on the chalkboard.

———— Lesson Content ————

Introduction

Sing "The Handwriting Song."

Skill Development

Demonstrate the formation of uppercase and lowercase cursive *r*—Verbalize the direction of the strokes as you write each letter on the chalkboard. Choose several volunteers to write the letters as you verbalize the strokes again.

**Swing up and drop,
Retrace and swing
 around to lock,
Drop right and curve.**

**Swing up,
Slide right,
Drop and curve.**

Demonstrate the writing of lowercase *r* in pairs.

Demonstrate the connecting of the letters in words—Write the following riddle on the chalkboard, pointing out that both the uppercase and lowercase letters connect to the letters that follow them. Call attention to the word *for.* Demonstrate the connection of the *o* and *r*.

Railroad crossing, look out for the cars. Can you spell that without any *r*s?

(Answer: Yes, that *is spelled* t-h-a-t. That *is always spelled without any* rs.)

Guided Practice

Direct the completion of worktext page 72—Read the instructions. Tell the students to trace the railroad track the train will ride along. Choose volunteers to name the roads in the order they are crossed. As the students complete the page, check for correct posture, paper position, and pencil hold.

Optional Activity

Direct an art activity—Tell the students to draw an imaginary railroad station on construction paper. Instruct them to draw and label the following signs in cursive writing for the station:

R.R. Station	*Tickets*	*Crossing*
Snack Shop	*Baggage*	*Restrooms*
Telephone		

Lesson 79   Tongue Twisters

Materials and Preparation

Have available:

• Handwriting paper for each student.

Prepare:

• The following tongue twisters in cursive on the chalkboard.

Peter pesters patient pink peacocks.

Ring-tailed raccoons race roaming rhinoceroses.

Prince Preston promised Princess Priscilla pretty primroses.

———— Lesson Content ————

Introduction

Create interest in today's lesson—Read the tongue twisters on the chalkboard. Encourage the class to repeat them. If time permits, allow the students to make up a few of their own.

Skill Development

Review the formation of uppercase and lowercase *p* and *r*—Verbalize the direction of the strokes as you write each letter on the chalkboard. Call attention to the word *Peter* as you remind the class that uppercase *p* does not connect to the lowercase letters that follow it. Allow several students to underline the *p*s and *r*s in the tongue twisters.

Guided Practice

Direct writing of tongue twisters—Tell the students to write the tongue twisters on handwriting paper. Instruct them to make up one of their own to write along with the others.

Optional Activity

Direct a writing activity—Write the following words and paragraph in cursive on the chalkboard. Tell the students to select the correct words from the list to complete the sentences as they write the paragraph.

marbles	hits	Rita	champion
ring	Carl	shoots	

Rita's friend _____ has a bag of _____. He lets _____ practice shooting his peppermint stripe marble. Rita _____ the marble into the _____. It _____ the other marbles, plink! Rita is a marble shooter.

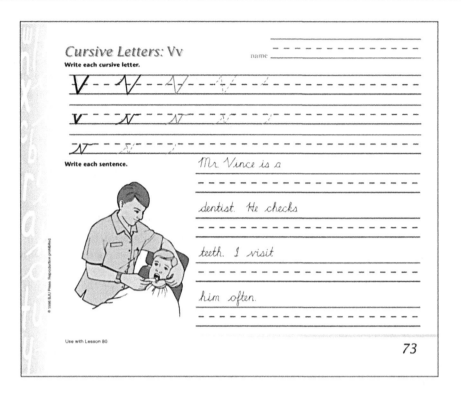

Materials and Preparation

Prepare:

- Handwriting lines on the chalkboard.
- The following sentence in PreCursive on the chalkboard.

Our dentist, David Pavro, lives in Vicksburg.

——— Lesson Content ———

Introduction

Lead a discussion about dentists—Ask the students to raise their hands if they have visited the dentist. Tell them the proper procedures for dental health: eating properly, brushing after meals, flossing, and having a yearly checkup by a dentist.

Skill Development

Demonstrate the formation of uppercase and lowercase cursive *v*—Verbalize the direction of the strokes as you write each letter on the chalkboard. Allow several students to write the letters on the chalkboard.

**Swing up,
Drop right,
Climb right.**

**Swing up,
Drop right,
Climb right,
Sweep out.**

Demonstrate the writing of lowercase *v* in pairs.

Demonstrate the connecting of the letters in words—Instruct a student to read the sentence on the chalkboard. Then write the sentence using cursive writing and point out that the uppercase letter *v* does not connect to the lowercase letters that follow it. Direct attention to the word *lives* and tell the students to note the way the letters *v* and *e* are connected. Allow several students to practice writing the word *lives* on the chalkboard.

Guided Practice

Guide the completion of worktext page 73—Choose a student to read the directions and others to read the sentences in the exercise. Tell the students to compare PreCursive and cursive *v*. Instruct them to complete the page independently.

Optional Activity

Direct a writing activity—Write the list below on the chalkboard. As you read the words aloud, tell the students to choose foods that are good for their teeth. Instruct the class to write these words on handwriting paper.

veal	*lollipops*	*cake*	*vegetables*
milk	*soda pop*	*cookies*	*caramel apples*
chicken	*vitamins*	*bananas*	*licorice*

Materials and Preparation

Have available:

- The poem "Writing Time" on chart paper.

Prepare:

- Handwriting lines on the chalkboard.
- The following sentence in PreCursive on the chalkboard.

  Xavier's x-rays were mixed up with Alex's x-rays.

——— Lesson Content ———

Introduction

Read the poem "Writing Time" in unison.

Skill Development

Demonstrate the formation of uppercase and lowercase cursive *x*—Verbalize the direction of the strokes as you write each letter on the chalkboard. Point out that the Pre-Cursive *x* is visible in the cursive letter.

(1) **Swing up,**
   Drop right and curve.
(2) **Drop left.**

(1) **Swing up,**
   Drop right and curve.
(2) **Drop left.**

Demonstrate the connecting of the letters in words—Instruct a student to read the sentence on the chalkboard. Write the sentence in cursive and point out that both the uppercase and lowercase *x* connect to lowercase letters. Call attention to the words *Xavier's* and *mixed*. Point out to the students that the second stroke of the letter *x* is added after the word is written. Allow time for several students to write the words on the chalkboard.

Guided Practice

Guide the completion of worktext page 74—Choose a volunteer to read the directions and the verse. Circulate among the students as they complete the page.

Optional Activity

Direct writing of a verse—Remind the students that our example is the Lord Jesus Christ. Tell them to write John 13:15 on handwriting paper.

A Friendly Letter

name _____

April 30
Dear Beth,
    Camping is fun. A raccoon
sleeps in the trash can!
I'll be home soon.
          Love,
          Irene

Write the letter in cursive writing.

Use with Lesson 82.

75

Materials and Preparation

Prepare:

- The following letter in cursive on the chalkboard.

 May 16

 Dear Jeff,

 I hope you like your new house. Dad said we could stop to see you on the way to Grandpa's. Wouldn't that be fun?

 Your friend,

 Keith

- The words *date, greeting, body,* and *closing* in cursive on the chalkboard.

———— Lesson Content ————

Introduction

Discuss the parts of a friendly letter—Direct attention to the letter written on the chalkboard. Choose a student to read it to the class. Instruct volunteers to read the words that name the parts of a friendly letter and to draw a line from the words to the parts they name.

Skill Development

Review the formation of uppercase and lowercase *p, r, v,* and *x*—Verbalize the direction of the strokes as several students write the letters on the chalkboard. Instruct the students to practice writing pairs of the letters *p* and *r*.

Guided Practice

Guide the completion of worktext page 75—Choose a volunteer to read the instructions and the letter. As students work on the page, walk around the classroom, giving encouragement and helping with spacing and indentations.

Optional Activity

Direct writing of a letter—Tell the students to write a letter to their parents, telling about things they have done at school.

Lesson 83   Addressing an Envelope (an assessment) Worktext page 76

Addressing an Envelope   name

Return Address
Irene Pope
Camp Maranatha
Hope, RI 02831

Address
Miss Beth Vick
10 Avis Road
Rice, VA 23966

Address the envelope. Use your best cursive writing.

Use with Lesson 83

76

Materials and Preparation

Prepare:

- A drawing of a large envelope on the chalkboard. Write the following addresses beside it.

From: Dave Levitt
Ash Road
Vernon, Vermont 05354
To: Patrick McRae
18 Seventh Street
Polk, Ohio 44866

———— Lesson Content ————

Introduction

Sing "The Handwriting Song."

Skill Development

Discuss correct form for addressing an envelope—Direct attention to the addresses on the chalkboard. Choose a volunteer to read them aloud. Write the addresses in the correct form on the envelope, verbalizing the placement of each line and the punctuation needed.

Assessment

Direct the completion of worktext page 76—Read the letter Irene wrote to Beth yesterday. Direct attention to Irene's address. Remind the students that the return address should be written in the top left-hand corner of the envelope and that Beth's address should be written in the center of the envelope. Tell the students to read the addresses one line at a time as you explain the abbreviations, capitalizations, and punctuation. Remind the students to use their best handwriting as they address the envelope.

Optional Activity

Direct a writing activity—Instruct the students to pretend that their handwriting paper is an envelope. Using correct placement, the students should use their own return address and "send" the envelope to the following address:

Mr. Tim Time

Ticker Road

Clockville, Timeland 12345

Lesson 84   Writing to a Missionary

Materials and Preparation

Have available:

- Several missionary prayer cards.
- An envelope and a postage stamp.
- Information about a specific missionary family with a child approximately the same age as your students and an envelope addressed to the missionary child.

Prepare:

- Handwriting lines on the chalkboard.

──── Lesson Content ────

Introduction

Display the missionary prayer cards—Sing a missionary song. Allow volunteers to read the names of the missionary families represented on the prayer cards. Ask what a missionary is and does. Ask the class if they can be missionaries right now. Lead a short discussion about missionary work that they can do. Show the addressed envelope and tell the children all you can to develop interest in the specific missionary child you have chosen.

Skill Development

Lead the class in writing a friendly letter—Instruct students to suggest sentences for a letter to a missionary child. Write the letter on the chalkboard or chart paper.

Guided Practice

Guide writing of a letter—Tell the students to write the letter that is on the chalkboard on handwriting paper. Choose the best one to send to the missionary child.

Optional Activity

Direct writing of a verse—Instruct the students to write the last portion of Isaiah 6:8 on handwriting paper.

"Then said I, Here am I; send me."

Cursive Letters: Ww   name _____

Write each cursive letter.

W — W — W — W — W

w — w — w — w — w

Read the poem.

Winter

Winter winds begin to blow
Covering all the ground with snow.
Coats and mittens, scarves and hats,
Skis and skates and fireside chats,
Signs of winter, Christmas cheer,
Usher in a brand-new year.

Underline the words that have the letter w. Write those below.

Winter   *blow*   *snow*

winds   *with*   *new*

Use with Lesson 85.

77

Materials and Preparation

Prepare:

- The names of the seasons on the chalkboard.
- Handwriting lines on the chalkboard.
- The following sentence in PreCursive on the chalkboard.

  Wendy wishes it were always winter.

———— Lesson Content ————

Introduction

Lead a discussion about seasons—Tell the students that a season is one of the four parts of the year. Choose a volunteer to read the names of the seasons written on the chalkboard. Read the phrases below. After each phrase is read, have students stand as soon as they can identify the season that the phrase tells about.

1. Colored leaves and chilly nights
2. Shade trees and ice-cold lemonade
3. Mittens, muffs, and balls of snow
4. Budding trees and warm sunshine

Allow time for students to name their favorite season. Tell the class that the letter they will study today is the first letter in the name of one of the seasons. Let them guess the letter.

Skill Development

Demonstrate the formation of uppercase and lowercase cursive *w*—Verbalize the direction of the strokes as you write each letter on the chalkboard. Point out that the Pre-Cursive letters are visible in the cursive letters.

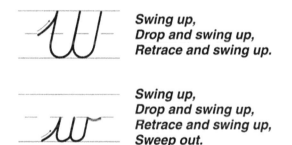

Swing up,
Drop and swing up,
Retrace and swing up.

Swing up,
Drop and swing up,
Retrace and swing up,
Sweep out.

Demonstrate the writing of lowercase *w* in pairs.

Demonstrate the connecting of the letters in words—Instruct a student to read the sentence on the chalkboard. Then write the sentence in cursive and point out that uppercase *w* does not connect to the lowercase letters that follow it. Call attention to the way the lowercase *w* connects to other lowercase letters. Allow several students to write the words *wishes* and *winter* on the chalkboard.

Guide the completion of worktext page 77—Tell a volunteer to read the directions at the top of the page. After the students complete the first three lines, draw attention to the poem "Winter." Allow a student to read the poem aloud. Ask another student to read the directions. Help the students locate the words containing the letter *w*. Allow the students to underline them as volunteers read the words. Direct the class to write the words on the lines.

Optional Activity

Direct a writing activity—Remind the students of the rules for adding -*s* and -*es* to words to make them plural. Write the following words on the chalkboard or chart paper. Instruct the students to write the plural form of each word on handwriting paper.

snowflake	*wish*	*snowstorm*
wind	*wreath*	*peach*
fox	*rain*	*turkey*

Lesson 86   Rules

Materials and Preparation

Have available:

- A picture of a clock.
- The Timothy Time puppet.

Prepare:

- The following in cursive on the chalkboard.

Clock Care

1. Shine the clock's face with a soft cloth.

2. Follow the directions for winding the clock.

3. Have a clock repairman clean the inside.

- Handwriting lines on the chalkboard.

———— Lesson Content ————

Introduction

Create interest in today's lesson—Use Timothy Time to pretend to clean the picture of a clock. Read the rules for clock care on the chalkboard to the class. Discuss reasons for each rule. Write *Pencil Care* on the chalkboard. Discuss rules that apply to proper use and care of pencils. Include the ones listed below in your discussion. As students suggest rules, write their ideas on the chalkboard.

Hold your pencil properly.

Sharpen your pencil correctly.

Do not chew on the pencil or eraser.

Put your name or initials on your pencil.

Have a special place to store your pencil when not using it.

Skill Development

Review the formation of uppercase and lowercase *w*—Verbalize the direction of the strokes as you write each letter on the chalkboard.

Guided Practice

Direct a rule-writing activity—Tell the students to write the rules for "Clock Care" on handwriting paper.

Optional Activity

Direct a matching activity—Write the lists below on the chalkboard. Tell the students to match the first part of the sentence to the correct second part. Instruct the class to write the complete sentences on handwriting paper.

Book Care

A	B
Wash hands	*or scribble on the pages*
Do not write	*in a bookcase.*
Store books	*or tear pages.*
Do not bend	*before opening a book.*

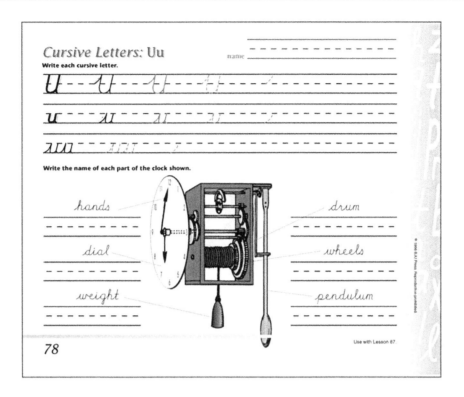

Cursive Letters: Uu   name _____

Write each cursive letter.

Write the name of each part of the clock shown.

hands

dial

weight

drum

wheels

pendulum

78   Use with Lesson 87.

Materials and Preparation

Prepare:

- Handwriting lines on the chalkboard.
- The following sentence in PreCursive on the chalkboard.

Andy Upton ran under the blue umbrella.

———— Lesson Content ————

Introduction

Sing "The Handwriting Song."

Skill Development

Demonstrate the formation of uppercase and lowercase cursive *u*—Verbalize the direction of the strokes as you write each letter on the chalkboard. Point out that the Pre-Cursive letter is visible in the cursive letter.

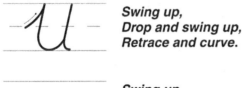

**Swing up,
Drop and swing up,
Retrace and curve.**

**Swing up,
Drop and swing up,
Retrace and curve.**

Demonstrate the writing of lowercase *u* in pairs.

Demonstrate the connecting of the letters in words—Instruct a student to read the sentence on the chalkboard. Write the sentence in cursive and point out that both the uppercase and lowercase *u* connect to lowercase letters. Allow several students to practice writing *blue* on the chalkboard.

Guided Practice

Guide the completion of worktext page 78—Direct a student to read the directions. Allow the students to complete the page independently.

Optional Activity

Direct a writing activity—Write the sentences below on the chalkboard. Tell the students to write the sentences, selecting the correct verbs to put in the blanks.

1. The four children (hang, hung) their coats on the pegs. *(hung)*
2. Curt is going to (build, built) a fort. *(build)*
3. Stuart (swing, swung) on the vine until it broke. *(swung)*
4. Lou (bring, brought) a tuba to music class. *(brought)*

99

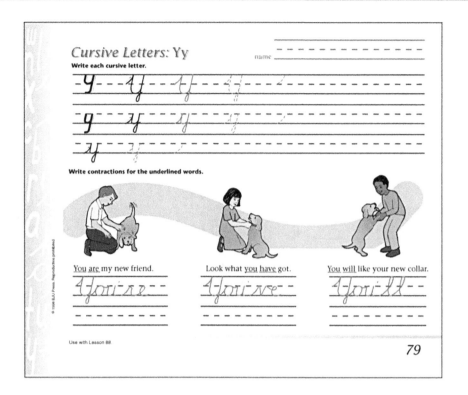

Materials and Preparation

Prepare:

- The lists below in cursive on the chalkboard.

you are	*you've*
you have	*don't*
you will	*isn't*
do not	*you're*
you had	*you'll*
is not	*you'd*

- The sentence below in PreCursive on the chalkboard.

  Yvonne is playing in the yard.

- Handwriting lines on the chalkboard.

—————— Lesson Content ——————

Introduction

Generate interest with a matching game—Elicit the definition of a contraction (a shortened form of two words in which one or more letters have been left out and an apostrophe put in the place of the omitted letter or letters). Explain that putting two words together as in the word *you're* does not change the meaning of the words *you are*. Direct the students' attention to the words on the chalkboard and have volunteers draw lines to match the words with the contractions.

Skill Development

Demonstrate the formation of uppercase and lowercase cursive *y*—Verbalize the direction of the strokes as you write each letter on the chalkboard.

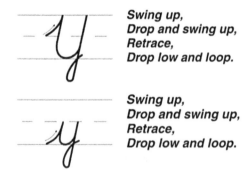

Swing up,
Drop and swing up,
Retrace,
Drop low and loop.

Swing up,
Drop and swing up,
Retrace,
Drop low and loop.

Demonstrate the connecting of the letters in words—Instruct a student to read the sentence on the chalkboard. Then write the sentence in cursive and point out that both the uppercase and lowercase *y* connect to the lowercase letters that follow them.

Guided Practice

Guide the completion of worktext page 79—Choose a volunteer to read the instructions. As the students trace the gray and dotted line guides, repeat the direction of the strokes. Instruct several students to read the sentences in the contraction exercises, substituting the contractions for the words. Let the students complete the page.

Optional Activity

Direct writing of contractions—Encourage the students to choose five of the contractions on the chalkboard to use in sentences. Tell them to write the sentences in cursive.

Lesson 89   Cursive Letters: *Zz*   Worktext page 80

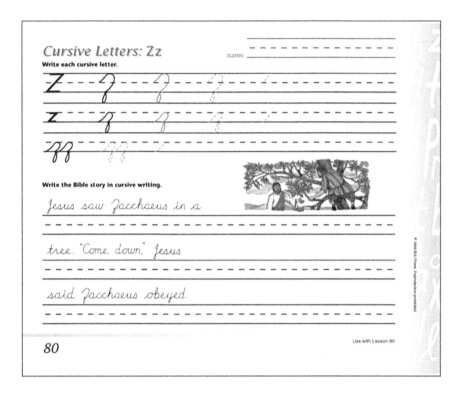

Materials and Preparation

Prepare:

- Handwriting lines on the chalkboard.
- The following sentence in PreCursive on the chalkboard.

  The lazy bee buzzed in Zeke's ear.

——— Lesson Content ———

Introduction

Generate interest with a colonial alphabet rhyme—Explain to the class that long ago children learned their letters for reading and writing from an alphabet poem. Every letter had its own rhyme. The first one said:

> A In Adam's fall
>   We sinned all.

Ask the class to guess the Bible character that might have taught the letter *z*. Give several hints until someone guesses correctly. Write the word *Zacchaeus* on the chalkboard.

Skill Development

Demonstrate the formation of uppercase and lowercase cursive *z*—Verbalize the direction of the strokes as you write each letter on the chalkboard. Direct several students to follow your example.

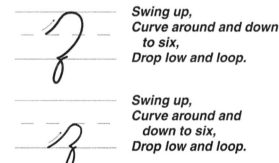

Swing up,
Curve around and down
*   to six,*
Drop low and loop.

Swing up,
Curve around and
*   down to six,*
Drop low and loop.

Demonstrate the writing of lowercase *z* in pairs.

Demonstrate the connecting of the letters in words—Instruct a student to read the sentence on the chalkboard. Then write the sentence in cursive and point out that both the uppercase and lowercase *z* connect to the lowercase letters that follow them. Allow several students to practice writing the words *buzzed* and *Zeke* on the chalkboard.

Guided Practice

Guide the completion of worktext page 80—Choose ten students to read the verses from Luke 19:1-10. Tell the class to complete the page independently.

Optional Activity

Direct a composing activity—Allow the students to write several sentences about their favorite Bible character.

Lesson 90   An Invitation (a review)   Worktext page 81

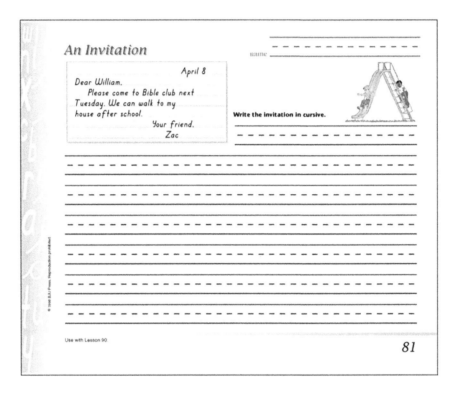

An Invitation

April 8

Dear William,
   Please come to Bible club next Tuesday. We can walk to my house after school.
           Your friend,
           Zac

name

Write the invitation in cursive.

Use with Lesson 90.

81

Materials and Preparation

Have available:

• The poem "Writing Time."

Lesson Content

Introduction

Read the poem "Writing Time."

Skill Development

Review the formation of the *w*, *u*, *y*, and *z*—Verbalize the direction of each stroke as several students practice writing the letters on the chalkboard. Then dictate the words *west*, *zip*, *yes*, *will*, *use*, and *wall* for students to practice joining *w*, *u*, *y*, and *z* with other letters.

Guided Practice

Discuss invitations—Ask whether any of the students have ever received an invitation to a party. Tell the students to write the invitation on the worktext page using their best handwriting.

Optional Activity

Direct an illustrating and composing activity—Tell the children to fold a piece of construction paper in half to look like a card. Instruct them to decorate the card and to write on the inside an invitation to a school event for a friend or relative.

A Bible Verse
Write Ephesians 6:1-2 in cursive writing.

name _____

Children, obey your parents in the Lord:
for this is right.
Honour thy father and mother;
which is the first commandment with promise.
Ephesians 6:1-2

82

Use with Lesson 91.

Materials and Preparation

Have available:

- Handwriting paper for each student.

——— Lesson Content ———

Introduction

Sing "Trust and Obey"—Discuss obedience to the Lord and to parents. Instruct the class to name Bible characters who were obedient.

Assessment

Direct the completion of worktext page 82—Choose a student to read the directions. Instruct the class to use their best handwriting as they write the verse on handwriting paper.

The exercises on worktext pages 82-94 are to be written on handwriting paper.

Optional Activity

Direct a writing activity—Instruct the students to write the chorus of "Trust and Obey" on handwriting paper.

Trust and obey,
For there's no other way
To be happy in Jesus,
But to trust and obey.

Materials and Preparation

Have available:

- The students' pretests from Lesson 47.
- Handwriting paper for each student.

—— Lesson Content ——

Introduction

Sing "The Handwriting Song."

Posttest

Direct a posttest—Distribute handwriting paper and direct the students to write in cursive the uppercase and lowercase letters of the alphabet.

Guide the students in contrasting the pretest and posttest—Before collecting the papers, distribute the pretest and encourage each student to note his own improvement in handwriting.

Optional Activity

Direct a writing activity—Tell the students to write the sentence below in cursive. Explain to them that every letter in the alphabet can be found in the sentence.

The quick red fox jumps over the lazy brown dog.

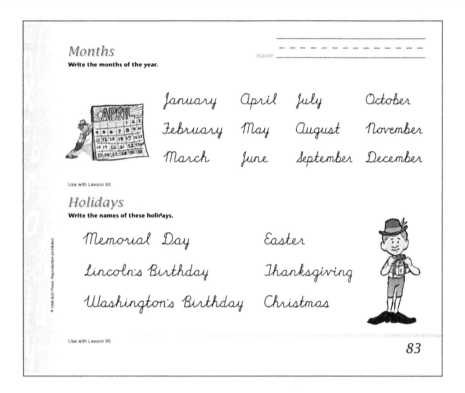

Materials and Preparation

Have available:

- A large calendar.
- Handwriting paper for each student.

Prepare:

- Handwriting lines on the chalkboard.

—————— Lesson Content ——————

Introduction

Create interest in today's lesson—Show the class a trick that will help them remember the number of days in each month. Have the students make their hands into fists. Each knuckle stands for a month with 31 days. Each indentation between knuckles stands for a month with 30 or less days. The first knuckle at the base of the index finger stands for January. It has 31 days. The first indentation between knuckles stands for February with 28 or 29 days, and then March is on the middle finger's knuckle, which stands for 31 days. Continue the same way until all the months are accounted for, starting over at the index finger every time you reach the end of your hand.

Skill Development

Review the formation of uppercase and lowercase *c, a,* and *o*—Point out the starting position and the direction of the strokes as you write each letter on the chalkboard. Allow several students to practice writing pairs of the lowercase letters on the chalkboard.

Guided Practice

Guide the completion of worktext page 83a—Before the children write the months of the year on handwriting paper, write the words *hot cocoa* and *icy lemonade* on the chalkboard. Ask a volunteer to find a month in the calendar when he would drink hot cocoa. Write that month under the words *hot cocoa.* Continue until several months between September and March are named (depending on the area in which your school is located). Ask what months are best for drinking icy lemonade. Tell students to show the months one at a time on the calendar. Write them on the chalkboard under *icy lemonade.* Recite the months in order as a class. Instruct the children to use the models in the textbook as a guide to write the months of the year. Remind them to capitalize the first letter of every month.

Optional Activity

Direct a writing activity—Encourage the students to write the paragraph below on handwriting paper, filling in the blanks:

> My birthday is in the month of ___. I will be ___ years old. The month before my birthday is ___, and the month after my birthday is ___. It is just ___ months away. I know because I have a ___ that has all the months of the year in it.

Lesson 94   Abbreviations

Materials and Preparation

Have available:

• Handwriting paper for each student.

Prepare:

• Handwriting lines on the chalkboard.
• The following list on the chalkboard.

June	Dec.	Aug.	May
Feb.	Nov.	Jan.	Apr.
Oct.	July	Mar.	Sept.

——— Lesson Content ———

Introduction

Discuss abbreviations—Elicit the definition of an abbreviation (the shortening of a word to save space). Ask students to give several examples of words that can be abbreviated. Direct the students' attention to the list on the chalkboard. Recite the full names of the months, pointing to each one in turn. Call attention to the use of capitalization and punctuation. Ask the class why some of the months are not abbrevi-

ated. Allow a volunteer to recite the months of the year in the correct order.

Skill Development

Demonstrate the formation of the cursive letter combinations *ar* **and** *or*—Verbalize the direction of the strokes as you write each letter on the chalkboard. Allow time for several students to practice writing the letter combinations on the chalkboard.

Guided Practice

Direct writing of abbreviations—Instruct the students to write the list from the chalkboard on handwriting paper. Tell the students to begin with Jan. and write the months of the year in the correct order.

Optional Activity

Direct a composing activity—Encourage the children to list the activities they can do now that they could not do a year ago. Begin the list by writing the following on the chalkboard:

1. I can write in cursive letters.

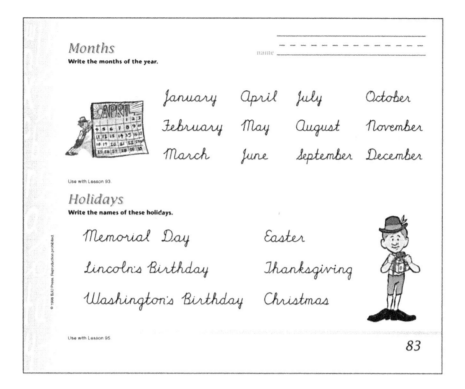

Materials and Preparation

Have available:

- A large calendar.
- A quarter, a penny, a valentine heart, and an American flag.
- Handwriting paper for each student.

Prepare:

- Handwriting lines on the chalkboard.

—————— Lesson Content ——————

Introduction

Create interest in today's lesson—Play a holiday game. Discuss the word *holiday* (a day when an important person is honored or a special day is remembered). Hold up the objects below that give a clue to a holiday. If no one is able to guess the holiday, give a verbal clue also. Write the name of each holiday on the chalkboard.

1. Quarter (the image of George Washington)—Washington's birthday is a holiday.
2. Valentine heart—Valentine's Day.
3. Penny (the image of Abraham Lincoln)—Lincoln's birthday is a holiday.

4. Flag—the Fourth of July and Flag Day.

Select a student to find these holidays on the calendar.

Skill Development

Review capitalization and punctuation rules—Remind the students that names of holidays begin with capital letters. Point out the use of the apostrophe and the break in the word before the *-s* is added to some words.

Review the formation of *q, g,* and *e*—Verbalize the direction of the strokes as you write each letter on the chalkboard. Write the words *quarter, heart, penny,* and *flag* on the chalkboard. Tell students to underline the *q*s, *g*s, and *e*s in the words.

Guided Practice

Guide the completion of worktext page 83b—Instruct the students to write on handwriting paper the names of the holidays listed on page 83. If necessary, remind them of the capitalization and punctuation rules.

Optional Activity

Direct a writing activity—Instruct the students to use a calendar to find five other holidays. Tell them to write the names of these holidays on handwriting paper.

Materials and Preparation

Have available:

- Handwriting paper for each student.

Prepare:

- Four or five pictures showing stages in plant growth.
- Handwriting lines on the chalkboard.

——— Lesson Content ———

Introduction

Create interest with a sequencing activity—Display several simple pictures showing stages in a plant's growth. Mix up the pictures and allow a student to put them in order as he describes what is happening to the plant.

Skill Development

Review the formation of uppercase and lowercase *g*—Verbalize the direction of the strokes as you write each letter on the chalkboard. Instruct several students to write the letters on the chalkboard.

Guided Practice

Guide the completion of worktext page 84a—Tell the students to write the observation report on handwriting paper. Check their posture, paper position, and pencil hold as they complete the activity.

Optional Activity

Direct a writing activity—Encourage the students to list the vegetables or fruits that grow or that they would like to have grow in their own gardens.

Lesson 97   Sequencing

Materials and Preparation

Have available:

- Handwriting paper for each student.

Prepare:

- Handwriting lines on the chalkboard.
- The following sentences on the chalkboard.

   Gerald bought some watermelon seeds.

   The plants produced ten big, juicy watermelons.

   Gerald planted the seeds.

   The plants grew.

   Gerald watered the seeds.

   The rain and sunshine made the seeds sprout.

——— Lesson Content ———

Introduction

Lead a sequencing activity—Direct the students' attention to the observations written on the chalkboard. Lead the class in discovering that the sentences are not sequenced correctly. Choose volunteers to number the sentences in the correct order.

Skill Development

Review the formation of uppercase and lowercase *g*—Verbalize the direction of each stroke as you write the letter on the chalkboard. Allow several students to write the letter on the chalkboard.

Guided Practice

Direct sequencing of sentences—Tell the students to write on handwriting paper the sentences from the chalkboard in the correct order.

Optional Activity

Direct a science and writing activity—Allow the students to plant seeds of their own in a Styrofoam cup. Tell them to watch the results closely and to make an accurate observation report.

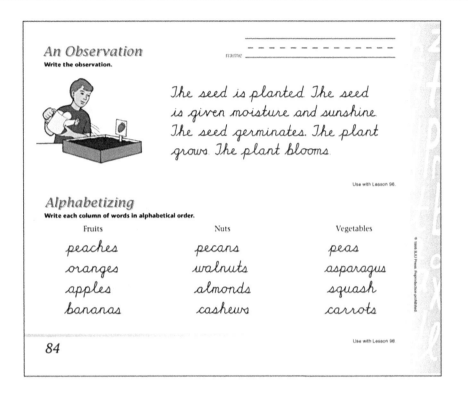

Materials and Preparation

Have available:

- Handwriting paper for each student.

Prepare:

- The words *rose, daisy, elm, birch, pansy, maple, tulip,* and *oak* in cursive on the chalkboard.
- The headings *tree* and *flower* in cursive on the chalkboard.

———— Lesson Content ————

Introduction

Conduct an alphabetizing activity—Choose eight students to categorize the words on the chalkboard as flowers or trees. Have one student at a time select a word and write it under the correct category. If time permits, allow the first student to write the word that comes first in alphabetical order in the list of his choice. Continue until both lists are alphabetized.

Skill Development

Review the formation of uppercase and lowercase *e*—Verbalize the direction of the strokes as you write each letter on the chalkboard. Choose several students to go to the list on the chalkboard to underline words containing the letter *e*.

Guided Practice

Guide the completion of worktext page 84b—Help the students to number the lists in alphabetical order. Instruct them to write the words in correct alphabetical order on handwriting paper.

Optional Activity

Direct a writing activity—Write the lists below on the chalkboard. Instruct the students to write and alphabetize the words in each list on handwriting paper.

    Grains: wheat, corn, barley, oats

    Trees: spruce, hemlock, pine, cedar

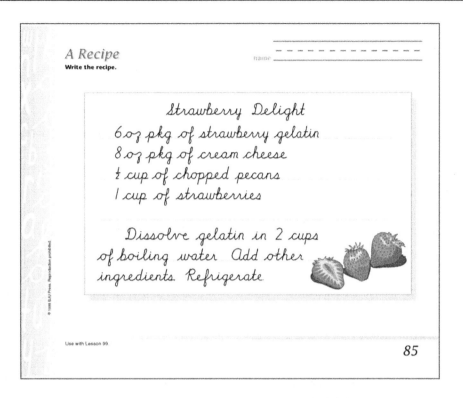

A Recipe
Write the recipe.

name

Strawberry Delight
6 oz pkg of strawberry gelatin
8 oz pkg of cream cheese
⅓ cup of chopped pecans
1 cup of strawberries

Dissolve gelatin in 2 cups
of boiling water. Add other
ingredients. Refrigerate.

Use with Lesson 99

85

Materials and Preparation

Have available:

- Ingredients for *Strawberry Delight* (found in the student text).
- Muffin paper for each student.
- Plastic spoon for each student.
- Handwriting paper for each student.

Prepare:

- The recipe *Strawberry Delight* in the muffin papers for each student.

———— Lesson Content ————

Introduction

Serve Strawberry Delight—Tell the students to use the plastic spoons to taste the Strawberry Delight. As the students try the dessert, ask what it tastes like. Write the descriptive words that the students suggest on the chalk-board. Ask the students if they can make the Strawberry Delight jiggle. Write the word *jiggle* on the chalkboard also.

Skill Development

Review the formation of uppercase and lowercase *i* and *j*—Verbalize the direction of the strokes as you write each letter on the chalkboard. Allow several students to write the letters and the word *jiggle* on the chalkboard.

Guided Practice

Guide the completion of worktext page 85—Instruct the children to write the recipe on handwriting paper.

Optional Activity

Direct a cutting and pasting activity—Encourage the students to cut recipes from magazines to paste onto index cards. If time permits, tell them to illustrate the dessert on the back of the index card.

Materials and Preparation

Have available:

- Recipes.

> If the optional activity from Lesson 99 was done, those recipes may be used today.

- Handwriting paper for each student.

Prepare:

- A favorite recipe of your own on the chalkboard.
- The following list of words on the chalkboard.

bread	*ham*	*peanut butter*	*mayonnaise*
butter	*jelly*	*bologna*	*cheese*

———— Lesson Content ————

Introduction

Create interest in today's lesson—Direct attention to the recipe on the chalkboard. Lead a contest allowing the children to make up names for your favorite recipe. Write their suggestions on the chalkboard. Allow students to read the titles of the recipes cut from magazines yesterday or the titles of those you have brought to class.

Skill Development

Review the formation of uppercase and lowercase *i* and *j*—Verbalize the direction of the strokes as you write each letter on the chalkboard. Allow several students to write words that contain *i* or *j* from the recipes used in the introduction.

Guided Practice

Direct writing of a recipe—Invite the students to write how they make their favorite kind of sandwich. Refer them to the word list on the chalkboard. Encourage them to put the steps in order and to include all of the needed ingredients. Circulate among the students to help them with spelling.

Optional Activity

Direct a drawing activity—Allow the students to paste their recipe to construction paper and to decorate the border.

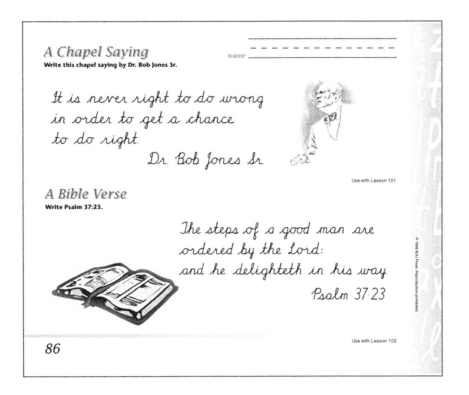

Materials and Preparation

Have available:

- Handwriting paper for each student.

Prepare:

- Handwriting lines on the chalkboard.

——— Lesson Content ———

Introduction

Generate interest with a story—Read the following story to the class:

Tony opened his book bag to get his lunch. As he lifted it out, he saw his brother Ricky's music book. "How did that get in there?" Tony whispered to himself.

"Please get in line quickly without talking," Mr. Thompson said.

Tony tucked the book under his arm and hurried outside to recess with the class.

As the children ran off in different directions to play, Tony leaned against the wall. No one was looking. He could sneak down the hall and leave the book in the piano room. No one would know he had broken the rules. And that way Ricky wouldn't get in trouble. Then Tony remembered the message he had heard in chapel. Mr. Case had quoted Dr. Bob Jones Sr.: "It is never right to do

wrong in order to get a chance to do right." He carried the book to his teacher.

"What have you got there?" Mr. Thompson asked.

"My brother Ricky's music book," Tony said. "I don't know what to do. He needs it for his piano lesson."

"Let me write you a note, and you may take it to his class in the junior high building," Mr. Thompson said.

Tony held the note tightly in one hand and Ricky's music book in the other. Just as he turned the corner, Ricky bumped into him.

"Tony, my book! I've been looking all over for it. Thanks."

Tony turned around and started back down the hall. "I'll have to tell Mr. Case that Dr. Bob was right," he thought as he stuffed the note in his pocket.

Skill Development

Review the formation of uppercase and lowercase *s*—Verbalize the direction of the strokes as you write each letter on the chalkboard. Instruct the students to line up in four or five rows at the chalkboard. As you repeat the stroke directions, have the first student in each row write the letter. Instruct the next student to check the letter and then write one himself as you repeat the stroke directions. As a reward you might allow the row with the neatest group of *s*s to erase the chalkboard.

Guided Practice

Guide the completion of worktext page 86a—Choose a volunteer to read the quotation. Instruct the students to use their best handwriting as they write the quotation on handwriting paper.

Optional Activity

Direct a composing activity—Encourage the students to write about an experience in which they did right instead of wrong.

Lesson 102   A Bible Verse   Worktext page 86b

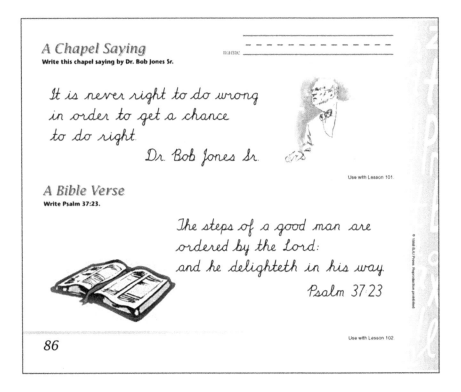

A Chapel Saying
Write this chapel saying by Dr. Bob Jones Sr.

name

It is never right to do wrong
in order to get a chance
to do right.
       Dr. Bob Jones Sr.

Use with Lesson 101.

A Bible Verse
Write Psalm 37:23.

The steps of a good man are
ordered by the Lord:
and he delighteth in his way.
       Psalm 37:23

Use with Lesson 102.

86

Materials and Preparation

Have available:

- Handwriting paper for each student.

Prepare:

- The following words and verse in cursive on the chalkboard.
  1. These four words inside footprint outlines—*good, ordered, Lord, delighteth.*
  2. Psalm 37:23, leaving out the four words *good, ordered, Lord,* and *delighteth.*
- Handwriting lines on the chalkboard.

——— Lesson Content ———

Introduction

Generate interest with a verse—Read the verse written on the chalkboard, pausing at the blanks. Choose four students to write the words from the footprints in the correct spaces. Read the verse in unison.

Skill Development

Review the formation of uppercase and lowercase *d*—Direct the students' attention to the footprint words. Help them discover the one letter that occurs in all four words (*d*). Write both forms of the letter *d* on the chalkboard, verbalizing the direction of each stroke.

Guided Practice

Guide the completion of worktext page 86b—Instruct the class to write the verse on handwriting paper.

Optional Activity

Direct a writing activity—Write "Thy God whom thou servest continually, he will deliver thee." (Daniel 6:16) on the chalkboard or on chart paper. Instruct the students to write the verse on handwriting paper.

Materials and Preparation

Have available:

- The Christian flag.
- Handwriting paper for each student.

——— Lesson Content ———

Introduction

Lead the class in the pledge to the Christian flag—Divide the class in half. Give a quiz, awarding a point for each correctly answered question. Use the following questions:

1. What does "pledging allegiance" mean? *(promising loyalty)*
2. What is liberty? *(freedom from sin)*
3. Name two things from the pledge that happened to our Savior. *(crucified, risen)*
4. What will Christ do someday? *(come again)*
5. Why is the cross in the Christian flag red? *(It stands for Christ's shed blood.)*
6. Whose kingdom does the Christian flag stand for? *(Christ's)*

7. Who will receive life and liberty according to the pledge to the Christian flag? *(all who believe)*

Skill Development

Review the formation of uppercase and lowercase *t*—Verbalize the direction of the strokes as you write each letter on the chalkboard. Point out the similarity between the letter *t* and the cross, using this rhyme:

> Sometimes when I write a letter *t*
> It makes me think of Calvary.

Guided Practice

Guide the completion of worktext page 87—Tell the students to write the pledge to the Christian flag on handwriting paper.

Optional Activity

Direct a writing activity—Tell the students to write several sentences on handwriting paper to tell how they were saved.

Materials and Preparation

Have available:

- Handwriting paper for each student.

Prepare:

- Stick puppets of Timothy Time's family. Glue magazine pictures to cardboard or construction paper and attach them to craft sticks. Include Father Time and his wife Frau or Mrs. Time, Grandfather and Grandmother Time, Uncle Franz, Tante or Aunt Bette, and Baby Fritz.

- Handwriting lines on the chalkboard.

———— Lesson Content ————

Introduction

Introduce Timothy Time's family—As you pretend to have Timothy Time introduce his family, write each name on the chalkboard. Explain the Swiss cultural background contained in the foreign names of Frau and Tante. Once all of them have been introduced, distribute the stick puppets among the students and tell them to find the name of the puppet you have given them on the chalkboard. Entitle the board "Timothy Time's Family."

Skill Development

Review the formation of uppercase and lowercase *f*—Instruct the students to tell you the first letter in the word *family*. Verbalize the direction of the strokes as you write each letter on the chalkboard. Tell students to underline the *f* in the names written on the chalkboard.

Guided Practice

Direct a writing activity—Tell the students to write the names of Timothy Time's family on handwriting paper.

Optional Activity

Direct a writing activity—Let the students list the people in their own families. If time permits, allow them to draw pictures of their families to make into stick puppets.

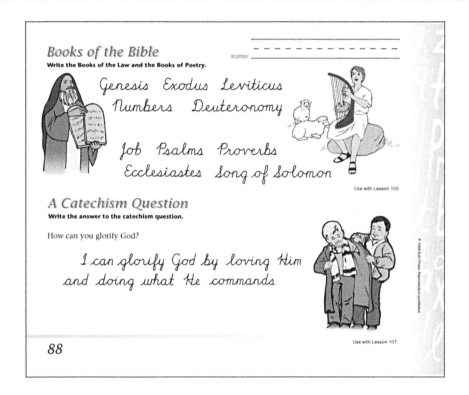

Materials and Preparation

Have available:

- Handwriting paper for each student.

Prepare:

- Handwriting lines on the chalkboard.

———— Lesson Content ————

Introduction

Create interest in today's lesson—Lead the students as they read aloud the books of the Old Testament listed in their Bibles. Choose volunteers who think they can say the five Books of the Law from memory to stand up and say them together. Write *Books of the Law* on the chalkboard. Ask the class whose law is given in these books. *(God's)* Point out that the Ten Commandments are God's law. Ask if anyone knows in which book of the Bible they are found. *(Exodus)* Tell the class that there are five Books of Poetry in the Old Testament and that the first one is Job. Direct students to stand if they think they can name one of the other four books

that come after Job. Let them recite the Books of Poetry. Write *Books of Poetry* on the chalkboard.

Skill Development

Review the formation of uppercase and lowercase *l*—Verbalize the direction of the strokes as you write each letter on the chalkboard. Ask if any of the Books of the Law have an *l* in them. Allow time for the students to look at the list of the books found in the front of their Bibles. Allow the student who finds *Leviticus* to write it on the board. Ask if the Books of Poetry have any *l*s in them. Allow other students to write *Psalms* and *Ecclesiastes* on the chalkboard.

Guided Practice

Guide the completion of worktext page 88a—Instruct the class to copy the Books of the Law and the Books of Poetry onto handwriting paper.

Optional Activity

Direct writing activities—Tell the students to find and write on handwriting paper five other books of the Bible that have the letter *l* in them.

Materials and Preparation

Have available:

- Handwriting paper for each student.

Prepare:

- Handwriting lines on the chalkboard.

——— Lesson Content ———

Introduction

Review the books of the Law and Poetry—Ask if anyone remembers the Books of the Law and Books of Poetry. Let several children recite them. Tell the class that there are twelve Books of History and that the first one is Joshua. Allow the students to name the rest one by one as you write them on the chalkboard. Label them *Books of History*.

Skill Development

Review the formation of uppercase and lowercase *b*—Verbalize the direction of the strokes as you write each letter on the chalkboard. Allow several children to write the word *book* on the chalkboard.

Guided Practice

Direct a writing activity—Instruct the students to copy the titles of the Books of History on handwriting paper. Remind them that the first letter of each word is capitalized.

Optional Activity

Direct a searching and writing activity—Tell the students that there are only six books in the Bible that have the letter *b* in the titles. Encourage the class to find and write them on handwriting paper.

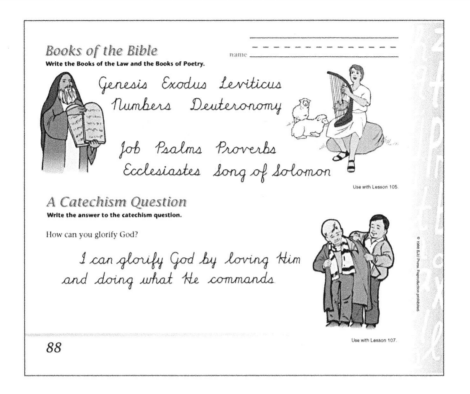

Materials and Preparation

Prepare:

- Handwriting lines on the chalkboard.
- The question *What is sanctification?* on the chalkboard.
- Handwriting paper for each student.

——— Lesson Content ———

Introduction

Create interest in today's lesson—Point out the catechism question on the chalkboard. Ask whether any students know the answer to the catechism. If a student knows the answer, allow the student to write the answer on the board. Otherwise, you may write the answer *(Sanctification is God's making me holy in heart and behavior.)* and help the students as they read the catechism question and answer.

Skill Development

Review the formation of uppercase and lowercase *h* and *k*—Verbalize the direction of the strokes as you write each letter on the chalkboard. Allow several students to come to the chalkboard and write the words from the catechism question that contain an *h* or *k*.

Guided Practice

Guide the completion of worktext page 88b—Tell the students to write the answer to the catechism question on handwriting paper.

Optional Activity

Direct a writing activity—Tell the students to write a catechism question on handwriting paper. Direct them to exchange papers with a friend and to answer each other's questions.

A Hymn   name

Write the first stanza of "Holy Bible, Book Divine".

Holy Bible, book divine.
Precious treasure thou art mine:
Mine to tell me whence I came.
Mine to teach me what I am.

Use with Lesson 108.

89

Materials and Preparation

Have available:

- The words to the hymn "Holy Bible, Book Divine."
- Handwriting paper for each student.

Prepare:

- Handwriting lines on the chalkboard.

——— Lesson Content ———

Introduction

Sing "Holy Bible, Book Divine"—Lead the class in singing the first and fourth stanzas of the hymn. Discuss the message of the song and the way students can make the Bible "their own" as the words suggest. Remind the children of the importance of reading and memorizing the book God gave to them.

Skill Development

Review the formation of uppercase and lowercase *n* and *m*—Verbalize the direction of the strokes as you write each letter on the chalkboard. Allow several students to write pairs of the lowercase letters on the chalkboard.

Guided Practice

Guide the completion of worktext page 89—Choose a volunteer to read the instructions. Circulate among the students to check their letter formation.

Optional Activity

Direct a writing activity—Tell the students to write on handwriting paper their favorite hymn from their Bible worktext. Compile these into a class hymnal.

120

Materials and Preparation

Have available:

- Handwriting paper for each student.

Prepare:

- Psalm 112:1 in cursive on the chalkboard.
- Handwriting lines on the chalkboard.

——— Lesson Content ———

Introduction

Create interest in today's lesson—Discuss the word *psalm*. Write the word *psalm* on the chalkboard. Instruct a student to find the dictionary meaning. Ask if any students have ever heard someone sing a psalm. If you know one, sing it to the class. ("The Lord Is My Shepherd" is a familiar one.)

Skill Development

Review the formation of uppercase and lowercase *p* and *r*—Verbalize the direction of the strokes as you write each letter on the chalkboard. Dictate the following words to several students, having them write the words on the chalkboard:

praise   glory   rejoice   pray   hope

Guided Practice

Guide writing of a verse—Direct attention to the verse on the chalkboard. Instruct the class to write the verse on handwriting paper.

Optional Activity

Direct a writing activity—Tell the children to write one of their favorite verses from the book of Psalms on handwriting paper.

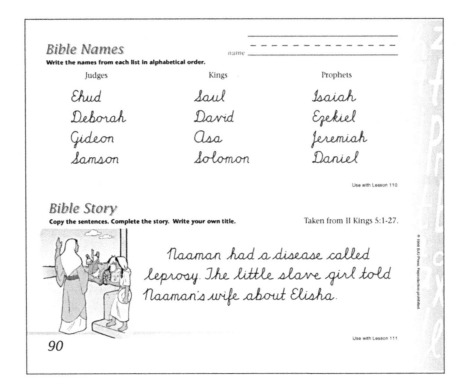

Materials and Preparation

Have available:

- Handwriting paper for each student.

Prepare:

- Several Bible characters' names on strips of paper.
- Handwriting lines on the chalkboard.

——— Lesson Content ———

Introduction

Play a Bible name game—Instruct all the students from the first row to come to the front of the class and choose a Bible name from the strips of paper prepared earlier. Direct them to alphabetize the names by standing in the correct order in a row. Continue with the other rows until everyone has participated.

Skill Development

Review the formation of uppercase and lowercase *v*—Verbalize the direction of the strokes as you write each letter on the chalkboard. Remind the students that uppercase *v* does not connect to the lowercase letters that follow it. Write the words *valley* and *David* on the chalkboard, demonstrating the correct way to connect lowercase *v* to letters following it in a word. Allow several students to write the word *David* on the chalkboard.

Guided Practice

Guide the completion of worktext page 90a—Instruct the students to number the lists in the correct alphabetical order; then direct them to write the words in alphabetical order on handwriting paper.

Optional Activity

Direct a composing activity—Tell the students to choose a favorite Bible character. Direct them to write a short paragraph telling what the character did. Point out that they can write about one of the characters used earlier in the lesson.

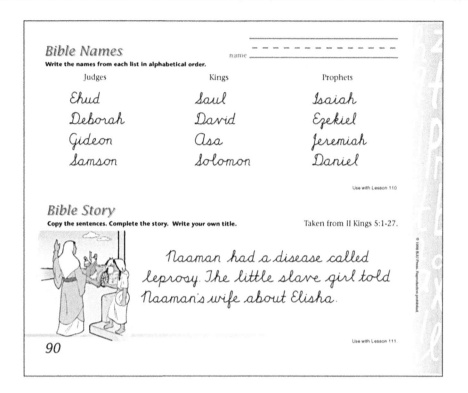

Materials and Preparation

Have available:

- Handwriting paper for each student.

Prepare:

- The following sentence in cursive on the chalkboard.

  Alex sneezed as Mother helped him into bed.

———— Lesson Content ————

Introduction

Compose a "round-robin" story—Discuss times when students received special care from parents and friends. Choose a student to read the sentence on the chalkboard. Direct the class in dictating sentences to make a "round-robin" story. Write the sentences on the chalkboard. Guide the students in choosing an appropriate title. Allow a volunteer to read the story aloud.

Skill Development

Review the formation of uppercase and lowercase *x*—Verbalize the direction of the strokes as you write each letter on the chalkboard. Write the word *xylophone*, demonstrating that the second stroke of the letter *x* is not written until all the letters in the word are written.

Guided Practice

Guide the completion of worktext page 90b—Choose a volunteer to read the beginning of the story. Instruct the class to write the sentences on handwriting paper and then to finish the story.

Optional Activity

Direct a composing activity—Tell the students to write and complete the following Bible story using their own words (based on Luke 17:11-19).

> The ten lepers ran to see Jesus. They wanted to ask Him to heal them. Soon they saw Him. "Jesus!" they called. The Lord Jesus turned to them.

A Poem
Copy this poem on your own paper.

name

Springtime

All the ice and snow have melted;
Now the tiny buds appear.
Bees are buzzing; birds are singing;
Happy Easter bells are ringing;
April rains bring lovely flowers.
All proclaim that spring is here.

Use with Lesson 112.

91

Materials and Preparation

Have available:

- Pussy willows and spring flowers or pictures of them.
- Handwriting paper for each student.

Prepare:

- Handwriting lines on the chalkboard.

——— Lesson Content ———

Introduction

Create interest in today's lesson—Display the pussy willows and flowers. Lead a discussion about pussy willows, showing how the little buds are soft as a pussycat's fur. Point out that the pussy willows and flowers are signs of spring. Encourage the class to name other signs of spring.

Skill Development

Review the formation of uppercase and lowercase *w*—Verbalize the direction of the strokes as you write each letter on the chalkboard. Allow two volunteers to write the words *pussy willows* and *flowers* on the chalkboard.

Guided Practice

Guide the completion of worktext page 91—Ask a student to read the poem "Springtime." Point out the signs of spring the poem tells about. Tell the class to write the poem on handwriting paper.

Optional Activity

Direct a composing activity—Tell the students to write a list of their favorite things to do in the springtime.

Lesson 113   Writing a Paragraph

Materials and Preparation

Have available:

- The Timothy Time puppet.
- Handwriting paper for each student.

Prepare:

- A model of a kite. On the tail write the words *up, up, up.*
- Handwriting lines on the chalkboard.

——— Lesson Content ———

Introduction

Lead a discussion about kites—Let Timothy Time pretend to fly the model of a kite. Call on a student to read the words on the tail of the kite. Allow the students to tell experiences that they have had with kites. If time permits, let the class fly a kite, or plan to fly one during recess or break time.

Skill Development

Review the formation of uppercase and lowercase *u*—Verbalize the direction of the strokes as you write each letter on the chalkboard. Allow several students to write the word *up* on the chalkboard.

Lead a discussion about paragraphs—Tell the students that a paragraph must be indented. Demonstrate indention by using cursive writing as you write the following paragraph on the chalkboard:

> *Way up in the sky my kite dips and turns with the wind. The birds whistle at it, but my kite never whistles back.*

Point out that all the sentences in a paragraph tell about the same thing.

Guided Practice

Direct a composing activity—Tell the students to write a paragraph about kite flying. Remind them of the discussion at the beginning of the lesson if they have difficulty in deciding what to write about.

Optional Activity

Direct an art activity—Encourage the students to design a model of a kite using construction paper. Let them write a message on the tail.

Materials and Preparation

Have available:

- Handwriting paper for each student.

Prepare:

- Handwriting lines on the chalkboard.

——— Lesson Content ———

Introduction

Direct a rhyming game—Divide the class into three teams. Tell each team to stand in a row and face the chalkboard. Above the first person on Team One write the word *shade*, above Team Two the word *trip*, and above Team Three the word *bat*. Give each team member an opportunity to write a word rhyming with the one on the chalkboard. The team with the most rhyming words wins.

Skill Development

Review the formation of uppercase and lowercase *y*—Verbalize the direction of the strokes as you write each letter on the chalkboard. Allow several students to write the letters on the chalkboard.

Guide the completion of worktext page 92a—Tell the students to number their papers from 1-6 on the front side and from 7-12 on the back. Instruct them to write each word from the top of page 92 on their paper. Then tell them to write a rhyming word for each word on their paper.

Optional Activity

Direct a composing activity—Allow the students to list some of their favorite things to do in the winter and to write a word that rhymes with each one.

Materials and Preparation

Have available:

- Handwriting paper for each student.

Prepare:

- Several sample puzzles. Glue magazine pictures to light cardboard and cut them into easy puzzle pieces.

- Handwriting lines on the chalkboard.

———— Lesson Content ————

Introduction

Lead a discussion about rainy days in the summer—Ask whether anyone has ever put together a puzzle on a rainy summer day. Pass out puzzles among every three or four children. As the students work them, discuss other rainy-day summer activities.

Skill Development

Review the formation of uppercase and lowercase *z*—Verbalize the direction of the strokes as you write each letter on the chalkboard. Write the word *puzzle* on the chalkboard. Allow several children to write the word *puzzle* on the chalkboard.

Guided Practice

Direct writing on handwriting paper—Begin the following story on the chalkboard. Tell the students to write and finish it.

> *Zeke opened the box. Inside was a puzzle. But the box had no picture.*

Optional Activity

Direct an art activity—Allow the students to make their own puzzles. Let them choose a picture to glue to a piece of cardboard or construction paper. Tell them to let the glue dry before they cut the picture into a puzzle.

Materials and Preparation

Have available:

- Handwriting paper for each student.

Prepare:

- Handwriting lines on the chalkboard.

——— Lesson Content ———

Introduction

Lead a discussion about summer vacations—Ask whether anyone will be going camping or on some other family trip during the summer. Mention other summer activities that the children may be planning.

Skill Development

Review the proper form for writing a paragraph—Remind the students that the first line of every paragraph is indented and that all the sentences in a paragraph talk about the same subject.

Guided Practice

Guide the completion of worktext page 92b—Tell the students to write the sentences and finish the story on handwriting paper.

Optional Activity

Direct a sequencing activity—Write the sentences below on the chalkboard. Instruct the students to put the sentences in proper sequence as they write them on handwriting paper.

Dad unrolled the sleeping bags.

We pitched the tent.

A raccoon crawled under the door and woke us up.

We looked for a camping spot.

We zipped the door closed and went to sleep.

A Poem
Write the poem.

name

Summertime

Is it summertime at last?
Now the days will fly too fast!
Days of camping, swimming, hiking,
Playing baseball games or biking—
Let's enjoy them while they're here.
Then remember them all year.

Use with Lesson 117

93

Materials and Preparation

Have available:

- Handwriting paper for each student.

Prepare:

- A favorite poem about summer in cursive on the chalkboard or on chart paper.

> A good source for poems is *Favorite Poems Old and New* by Helen Ferris.

──── Lesson Content ────

Introduction

Play a game—Divide the class into two baseball teams. Explain to the students that they can score a run for their team if they write the correct letter on the chalkboard. The team that is not batting pitches letters of the cursive or PreCursive alphabet one at a time to the batter. If the batter writes the letter correctly, he adds a run to his team's score. If he writes an incorrect letter or forms the letter improperly, his team makes an out.

Skill Development

Discuss correct poetry form—Direct attention to the summer poem on the chalkboard. Point out the capitalization of the first word of each line. Instruct the students to read the capitalized words. Point out the punctuation used in the poem.

Guided Practice

Guide the completion of worktext page 93—Choose a student to read the poem aloud. Instruct the class to write the poem on handwriting paper.

Optional Activity

Direct a writing activity—Discuss the activities mentioned in the poem. Instruct the students to write a short paragraph about summertime activities.

Lesson 118   Poetry Writing

Materials and Preparation

Have available:

- The Timothy Time puppet.
- The poem from yesterday's lesson.
- A nonrhyming poem.
- Handwriting paper for each student.

———— Lesson Content ————

Introduction

Create interest in today's lesson—Let the Timothy Time puppet pretend to read the poem from yesterday's lesson. Direct the class in reading it together a second time.

Skill Development

Discuss poetry form—Point out that every nonindented line in poetry is capitalized. Show the students that sentences are punctuated. Tell the students that not all poems rhyme. If time permits, read a nonrhyming poem to the class.

Guided Practice

Direct the students in writing a poem—Ask the following questions. Instruct the students to write the answers in complete sentences, one per line. Their answers will create a nonrhyming poem.

- ➤ What is your favorite food to eat in the summer?
- ➤ What does it taste like?
- ➤ How much could you eat?
- ➤ When do you like best to eat it?
- ➤ How do you feel when you have finished eating it?

Collect the poems. Correct errors and keep them for tomorrow's lesson.

Optional Activity

Direct an art activity using construction paper—Tell the students to illustrate their poems.

Materials and Preparation

Have available:

- Handwriting paper for each student.
- The students' poems from yesterday.

———— Lesson Content ————

Introduction

Create interest in today's lesson—Read several of the poems written yesterday. Make as many positive comments as possible.

Skill Development

Review poetry form—Give helpful hints concerning poetry form. Remind the students of capitalization and punctuation rules.

Guided Practice

Direct the students in writing a poem—Redistribute the children's poems from yesterday. Tell the students to correct mistakes on their papers and write a final draft. Emphasize the importance of neatness. Use these poems to compile a classroom anthology of poetry.

Optional Activity

Direct a writing activity—Instruct the students to write a poem by answering these questions:

1. What is your favorite game in the summer?
2. Where do you play?
3. Who plays with you?
4. What do you do when you play, or how do you play?

Pledge to the American Flag name _____

Copy the pledge to the American flag.

I pledge allegiance
to the flag
of the United States
of America and to
the republic for
which it stands,
one nation under God,
indivisible,
with liberty and
justice for all.

94

Use with Lesson 120.

Materials and Preparation

Have available:

- A dictionary.
- Handwriting paper for each student.

—————— Lesson Content ——————

Introduction

Lead a discussion about patriotism—Ask if anyone remembers what the word *patriot* means. Instruct a student to look up the word in the dictionary. See if the students can think of a way they can show they are patriotic. Explain that when they pledge allegiance to the flag, they promise to be loyal to their country. Select a student to look up the definitions for the words *republic, indivisible, liberty,* and *justice.* Stand as a class and say the "Pledge to the American Flag."

Guided Practice

Guide the completion of worktext page 94—Tell the students to write the "Pledge to the American Flag" on handwriting paper.

Optional Activity

Direct a writing activity—Write the information below on the chalkboard. Instruct a student to read it aloud. Direct the students to write the information on handwriting paper.

Our Flag

Each color in our flag has a special meaning. Red stands for courage, white for purity, and blue for justice. The design of our flag has a special meaning too. The thirteen stripes stand for the thirteen colonies that became the first thirteen states. The fifty stars stand for the fifty states of America.

I pledge allegiance to the flag because I am a loyal American.

Appendix

Bulletin Boards

You can learn to prepare good bulletin boards if you are willing to take the time. Design your bulletin boards to enrich the lessons in HANDWRITING 2 for Christian Schools, not just to decorate the walls of your classroom. Bulletin boards should attract attention and provide information. You should have, however, at least one bulletin board (or wall) on which you can display the children's art, compositions, or other work.

An attractive, informational bulletin board is created with more than construction paper and felt-tipped markers. Real objects, such as shells and tree limbs with leaves, create a stunning effect. Cut letters for captions from things like Styrofoam, sponge, cardboard, or fabric scraps. Use newspapers, a variety of textiles, tissue paper, or even wrapping paper for backgrounds. (Construction paper tears easily, fades, and usually has to be pieced.) To make the bulletin board look neat, pin materials onto it rather than staple them on. Let your imagination work for you. But remember to change your bulletin boards frequently.

You can easily enlarge the figures in the sample bulletin boards that follow or any picture you have by using the grid method of enlargement. Draw a grid of one-centimeter squares on the picture you wish to enlarge. Draw another grid on a separate piece of paper but enlarge the squares proportionately. For example, if you want your enlargement to be twice as large, make the squares two centimeters on each side. Copy the figure square by square onto the enlarged grid. Presto! You've become an artist.

Note: If you wish to reduce a picture, draw the larger grid on the original picture.

Time to Ring

N-N-N-NICE HANDWRITING

Something to *Hum* **About**

My Best

Handwriting

name

Use with Lesson 1.

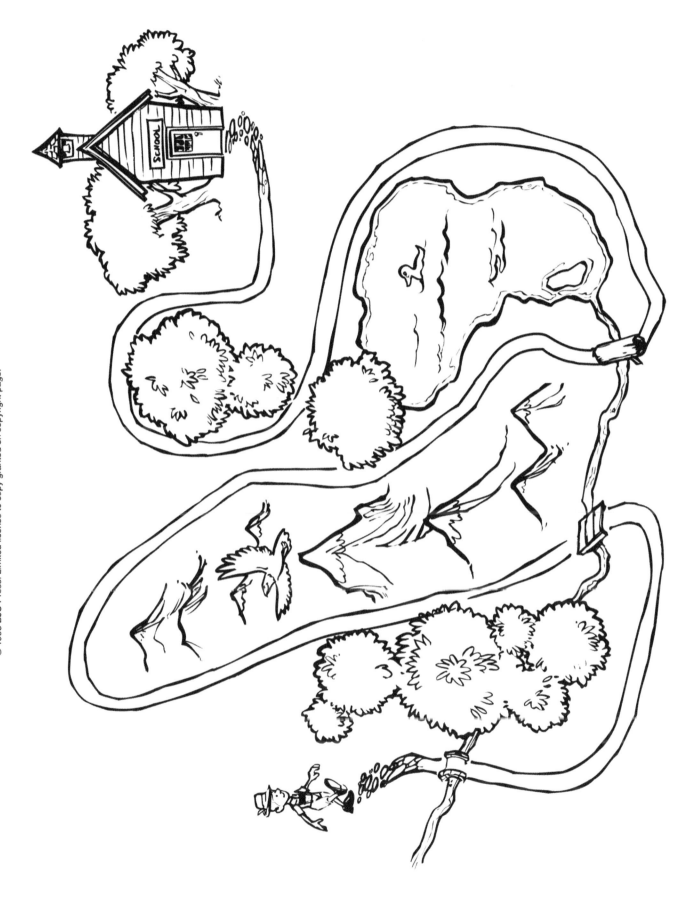

Use with Lesson 1.

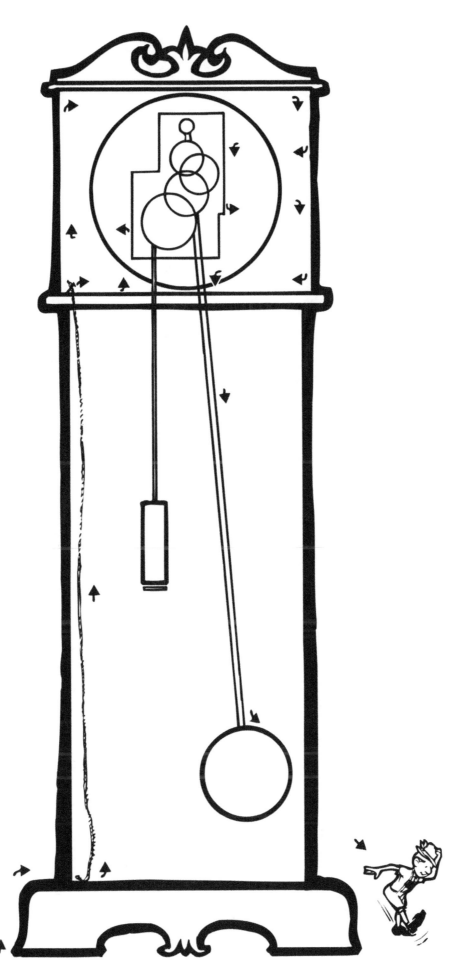

Appendix   Use with Lesson 3.   A13

Use with Lesson 6.

Use with Lesson 46.

An Evaluation

name

	Satisfactory	Shows improvement	Needs improvement	Suggestions for improvement
1. Posture				
2. Paper positioning				
3. Pencil hold				
4. Letter formation				
5. Alignment				
6. Slant				
7. Spacing				
8. Neatness				

The Handwriting Song

"The Handwriting Song," words and music, ©1982 BJU Press. All rights reserved.

Glossary

alignment—the correct placement of letters in relation to the baseline

baseline—the line on which the written letters rest

bounce—the ending of the stroke for the lowercase *f* and *q* that leads to the connecting of the cursive letter that follows

cursive stroke—the stroke that differentiates many PreCursive letters from their counterpart cursive letters; serves as the connecting stroke between most letters

curve—the ending of the stroke of most PreCursive and cursive letters

descenders—the portion of certain letters that descends below the baseline

loop—to cross a part of the letter already written with a high, sweeplike stroke

lowercase letters—uncapitalized letters

midline—the line of dashes found between the top line and baseline

one o'clock letters—letters beginning at the one o'clock position as compared to a clock; found in uppercase and lowercase *a, c, g, o, q,* and in uppercase *e*

retrace—backtracking along a part of the letter already written

rhythm—regularity of pressure patterns of fingers on the writing instrument

serif—a slight curve at the end of many letters

slant—a 5 to 15 degree tilt of letters

spacing—the amount of distance between letters and words and the arrangement of writing on the page

sweep out—the ending of a stroke that moves outward from left to right, connecting to letters that follow in a word; found in uppercase *b* and *i* and lowercase *b, o, p, s, v,* and *w*

top line—the uppermost portion of a handwriting line; the line above the midline

uppercase letters—capitalized letters